AUTOMATE THE BORING STUFF WITH PYTHON

Create 3D Games and Interactive Experiences from Scratch

THOMPSON CARTER

TABLE OF CONTENTS

INTRODUCTION

1. Welcome to Game Development with Unity

Game development is a fascinating field, one that combines art, storytelling, and technology to create interactive experiences that captivate and entertain people worldwide. Whether it's the feeling of exploring a vast open world, the rush of a fast-paced action game, or the challenge of a strategic puzzle, games have a unique power to engage. This book is here to guide you through the journey of creating games with Unity—a versatile, widely used game development engine that empowers both beginner and advanced developers alike.

In this book, you won't just learn how to use Unity; you'll also gain a deeper understanding of the game development process. We'll approach each topic with real-world examples and practical exercises to ensure that by the end, you're equipped with skills that translate into building your own games, not just replicating examples.

2. Why Unity? Understanding the Game Engine's Power and Flexibility

Unity has become one of the most popular game engines in the world, and for good reason. Unity provides a powerful and intuitive interface, a highly customizable development environment, and support for both 2D and 3D games. Whether you're an indie developer aiming to build a small mobile game or a professional working on a large project, Unity's flexibility makes it an ideal choice.

Here are some key reasons why Unity has been embraced by developers globally:

- **Cross-Platform Compatibility**: Unity supports over 25 platforms, including mobile, desktop, consoles, and VR/AR devices. This flexibility means you can reach a wide audience with minimal extra work.
- **Extensive Asset Store**: The Unity Asset Store provides a vast collection of pre-made assets, tools, and templates, making it easy to add everything from 3D models to special effects.
- **Intuitive Interface**: Unity's interface is designed to be approachable for beginners, yet powerful enough for advanced users. It offers a range of tools for designing, coding, and managing projects.
- **Thriving Community and Support**: With millions of users worldwide, Unity has an active community ready to share tutorials, assets, and advice. This supportive ecosystem ensures help is always available when you need it.

Throughout this book, you'll learn how to leverage these strengths, making Unity's powerful features work for you. By the end, Unity won't just be a tool you use—it will be a platform you understand and feel comfortable with, one that lets you express your creativity.

3. What This Book Covers: Breaking Down Game Development with Real-World Examples

Each chapter in this book builds on the previous one, starting with basic concepts and progressing to more advanced topics. Here's a quick overview of what you can expect:

- **Unity Interface and Setup**: We start with a guided tour of Unity's user interface, helping you become comfortable navigating the various panels and windows. You'll set up your first project and understand the different components that make up a Unity project.

- **Creating Game Worlds**: From adding objects and environments to working with lighting and sound, you'll learn how to bring your game world to life.

- **Scripting with C#**: Unity's scripting language, C#, is essential for creating interactive elements. We'll cover basic programming concepts in a way that's accessible even if you're new to coding.

- **Implementing Game Mechanics**: Game mechanics are the heart of any game. From controlling characters to adding physics, you'll learn to create gameplay that feels responsive and engaging.

- **User Interface (UI) and HUD Design**: A game's user interface guides players and enhances their experience. You'll learn to design intuitive interfaces and displays that provide essential information without distracting from gameplay.
- **Advanced Features**: For those ready to dive deeper, we'll cover multiplayer features, AI programming, and optimization techniques to improve your game's performance.

By using real-world examples—whether it's implementing enemy AI or building a simple inventory system—this book ensures that each chapter gives you practical skills you can apply immediately.

4. Who This Book Is For

This book is designed for anyone interested in learning game development with Unity, regardless of experience level. If you're new to programming or game design, you'll find step-by-step instructions and explanations that make complex concepts easier to understand. For experienced developers, this book will serve as a guide to Unity's advanced features, offering insights into efficient workflows and best practices.

Here's a breakdown of how readers at different levels can benefit:

- **Beginners**: If you've never written a line of code or touched a game engine before, you're in the right place.

Each chapter begins with foundational concepts, progressing gradually to ensure you don't feel overwhelmed.

- **Intermediate Developers**: If you're familiar with some game development concepts, you'll find value in the deeper dives into scripting, optimization, and game mechanics.
- **Experienced Developers**: Even seasoned developers will find Unity-specific insights and advanced workflows useful, especially if they're transitioning from another engine.

5. What Makes a Great Game? A Look at Core Game Design Principles

Before diving into Unity, let's consider what makes a game enjoyable. Understanding these core principles will help you design with purpose, aiming to create experiences that resonate with players.

- **Engaging Gameplay**: Successful games have compelling mechanics that keep players engaged, whether it's through challenges, rewards, or freedom to explore.
- **Intuitive Controls**: Games should feel responsive and easy to control, allowing players to focus on the experience rather than struggling with mechanics.
- **Aesthetic Appeal**: While graphics aren't everything, a visually appealing game enhances immersion. Unity's tools can help you create both realistic and stylized visuals.

- **Emotional Connection**: Games often tell stories or present challenges that evoke emotions, whether excitement, fear, or curiosity.

Unity is designed to help you achieve each of these qualities, but it's up to you, the developer, to decide how to bring them together in a way that feels cohesive.

6. The Journey from Idea to Game

Game development is a process. It's not just about learning a set of tools and techniques; it's about understanding how to turn a creative idea into a playable experience. Here are the stages you'll typically go through:

- **Conceptualization**: Defining your game's concept, mechanics, and audience.
- **Prototyping**: Building a basic version to test ideas and refine mechanics.
- **Development**: Building the game world, programming mechanics, and polishing the experience.
- **Testing**: Ensuring the game functions as intended and is enjoyable to play.
- **Publishing**: Releasing your game to the world.

This book follows this journey, providing insights and practical advice at each stage, so that by the end, you'll understand the complete lifecycle of game development.

7. Real-World Examples and Exercises: Hands-On Learning

Theory alone won't make you a skilled game developer. That's why this book emphasizes hands-on learning. In each chapter, you'll find practical exercises that reinforce what you've learned, along with real-world examples to show how professional developers approach similar challenges.

Here's what to expect:

- **Hands-on Exercises**: Step-by-step projects and coding exercises to solidify concepts.
- **Case Studies**: Examples from real games (both big-budget and indie) that illustrate how Unity's tools can be used in diverse ways.
- **Challenges**: At the end of some chapters, you'll find optional challenges designed to test your skills and push your creativity further.

8. Tips for Success and Staying Motivated

Learning game development is a marathon, not a sprint. It can feel overwhelming at times, especially when tackling new concepts or troubleshooting issues. Here are some tips to keep in mind as you work through this book:

- **Start Small**: Don't worry about creating the next blockbuster game immediately. Begin with small projects that focus on specific skills, and build from there.

- **Embrace Mistakes**: Bugs and errors are a natural part of the development process. Each one offers a learning opportunity.
- **Experiment and Explore**: Game development is as much an art as it is a science. Experiment with Unity's features, try new ideas, and don't be afraid to diverge from the book's examples.
- **Seek Feedback**: Show your work to others and listen to their feedback. Fresh eyes can often spot things you've missed.

Game development is both challenging and rewarding. By the end of this book, you'll not only have the skills to create games with Unity, but also the confidence to pursue your own projects and bring your unique ideas to life.

9. Let's Get Started!

Game development with Unity is a skill that will serve you well, whether you're aiming for a career in the industry or simply want to create games for fun. As you begin this journey, remember that learning is a process. Take it one chapter at a time, experiment, and enjoy the process. By the end, you'll have the skills and knowledge to create your own games, as well as the confidence to explore Unity's vast potential on your own.

In the next chapter, we'll start with the basics of Unity's interface and get your first project up and running. Let's dive in!

CHAPTER 1: INTRODUCTION TO PYTHON PROGRAMMING

Python is widely recognized as one of the most versatile and beginner-friendly programming languages available today. It's particularly well-suited for automating repetitive tasks, thanks to its readability, extensive libraries, and supportive community. This chapter introduces Python as a tool for automation, guides you through installing Python, setting up your environment, writing your first Python script, and provides real-world examples of Python applications.

Why Python is Ideal for Automation

Python's popularity in the tech world is no accident. Here are some of the key reasons why Python is ideal for automating tasks:

1. **Readability and Simplicity**:
   - Python's syntax is designed to be easy to read and understand, making it accessible for beginners. The language uses plain English keywords and avoids unnecessary complexity, allowing you to focus on problem-solving rather than getting bogged down by syntax.

2. **Extensive Libraries**:

- o Python has a rich ecosystem of libraries that provide functionality for almost any automation task imaginable. For example:
    - **os** for interacting with your computer's file system.
    - **requests** for web scraping and making web requests.
    - **smtplib** for sending emails.
    - **openpyxl** for automating Excel tasks.
- o These libraries allow you to automate complex tasks without having to write extensive code from scratch.

3. **Cross-Platform Compatibility**:
    - o Python is cross-platform, meaning it works on Windows, macOS, and Linux. This flexibility ensures that your scripts will run on various systems with minimal adjustments, making Python ideal for automating tasks on any machine.

4. **Community and Support**:
    - o Python's vast community and extensive documentation mean that solutions, tutorials, and support are just a search away. If you encounter a problem, there's a good chance someone else has already solved it and shared the solution.

5. **Efficient Workflow for Rapid Development**:

○ Python's concise syntax and powerful libraries allow you to develop and test automation scripts quickly, making it ideal for prototyping and implementing automation solutions on the go.

Installing Python and Setting Up Your Environment

Before writing Python code, you'll need to install Python and set up a coding environment.

1. **Download and Install Python**:
   ○ Visit Python's official website and download the latest version of Python.
   ○ Follow the installation instructions for your operating system. During installation, make sure to check the option **"Add Python to PATH"** (on Windows) to allow you to run Python from the command line.

2. **Verify the Installation**:
   ○ Once installed, open a command line interface (Command Prompt on Windows, Terminal on macOS/Linux) and type:

   bash
   Copy code
   python --version

o   You should see the installed Python version displayed. If you see an error, double-check your installation steps.

3. **Installing a Code Editor**:

   o   Python code can be written in any text editor, but using a dedicated code editor enhances productivity. Some popular choices are:

      ▪ **VS Code**: A free, highly customizable editor with Python support.

      ▪ **PyCharm**: A full-featured Python IDE with tools for debugging, testing, and project management.

      ▪ **Sublime Text**: A lightweight, fast editor with a large library of extensions.

4. **Setting Up Virtual Environments** (Optional but Recommended):

   o   Virtual environments allow you to manage packages independently for each project, avoiding version conflicts.

   o   To create a virtual environment, open your command line, navigate to your project directory, and run:

   bash
   Copy code
   ```
   python -m venv myenv
   ```

- o Activate the environment:
  - ▪ On Windows: myenv\Scripts\activate
  - ▪ On macOS/Linux: source myenv/bin/activate
- o Once activated, any packages you install will be specific to this environment.

Writing Your First Python Script

With Python installed, you're ready to write your first script!

1. **Open Your Code Editor** and create a new file called hello.py.
2. **Write a Simple Script**:
   - o Type the following code in your file:

   python
   Copy code
   print("Hello, world!")

   - o This is a simple script that tells Python to display "Hello, world!" on the screen.
3. **Running the Script**:
   - o Save your file and open your command line. Navigate to the folder containing hello.py, then type:

   bash
   Copy code

python hello.py

    o   If everything is set up correctly, you should see:

Copy code
Hello, world!

    o   Congratulations! You've just run your first Python script.

Real-World Examples of Python Applications

Now that you've written your first Python script, let's explore how Python is used in the real world to automate tasks across various fields. These examples highlight Python's power and flexibility:

1. **Automating File and Folder Organization**:
   - Python can be used to organize files on your computer. For example, you could write a script that automatically sorts files into folders based on file type (e.g., images, documents, videos).
   - This type of automation is particularly useful if you frequently download files or want to keep your desktop organized.

2. **Web Scraping**:
   - Python can be used to extract data from websites using libraries like **BeautifulSoup** and **requests**. For instance, you could scrape data from a news

website and compile the latest headlines in a text file.

- o Web scraping is commonly used for data collection, such as gathering prices from e-commerce sites or collecting research data from online sources.

3. **Email Automation**:

- o Python's **smtplib** library allows you to automate email sending. You could use it to set up automated email notifications or reminders, or even a daily summary email that compiles important information for you.

- o Many businesses use email automation scripts to send personalized responses, reducing the time spent on repetitive communications.

4. **Excel and Data Analysis**:

- o Python can automate Excel tasks and data analysis with libraries like **openpyxl** and **pandas**. For example, you could write a script that pulls data from multiple Excel files, analyzes it, and generates a summary report.

- o This is particularly useful in industries like finance and research, where working with large datasets is common.

5. **Game Development and Interactive Applications**:

- o Python is also used in game development, especially for prototyping and creating simple games or interactive applications with **Pygame**.
- o Developers use Python for quickly building and testing game mechanics or small educational games.

6. **Building Bots and Automated Customer Support**:
   - o With libraries like **Tweepy** (for Twitter) or the **discord.py** API, Python is widely used to create bots that interact with users, handle simple customer service tasks, or automate social media postings.
   - o This is useful for small businesses or individuals who want to automate responses to frequently asked questions or maintain an online presence.

7. **Data Visualization and Reporting**:
   - o Python's **matplotlib** and **seaborn** libraries allow users to create charts and graphs, automating the generation of reports or visualizations.
   - o This is commonly used in business intelligence, where Python scripts can pull data from databases, process it, and create visual reports automatically.

8. **Machine Learning and Predictive Analysis**:
   - o Python is the leading language for machine learning, thanks to libraries like **scikit-learn**, **TensorFlow**, and **Keras**. Machine learning models can predict

trends, classify data, and even generate recommendations.

○ For instance, you could create a simple recommendation system that suggests products based on user behavior, or predict future sales trends based on historical data.

Python is a powerful language with broad applications in automation, data analysis, web scraping, and more. In this chapter, you've set up Python, written your first script, and explored various ways Python is used in the real world. The foundations laid here will allow you to move confidently into automating practical tasks in the following chapters.

With Python ready on your computer, you're now set to dive deeper into the language and start learning automation techniques that will save you time and streamline everyday tasks.

CHAPTER 2: BASIC PYTHON SYNTAX AND CONCEPTS

Understanding basic syntax and foundational concepts is essential before diving into automation. This chapter covers core elements like variables, data types, operators, control structures (loops and conditionals), and functions. By the end, you'll apply these concepts to build a simple calculator program, giving you hands-on experience with Python's capabilities.

Variables, Data Types, and Basic Operators

Variables and data types are the building blocks of Python. Let's go through each of these fundamental concepts.

1. **Variables**:
    - A **variable** is a named storage location that holds data, which can be changed or reused throughout a program. Assigning a value to a variable is as simple as:

        python

```
Copy code
name = "Alice"
age = 30
```

- Here, name is assigned a string ("Alice"), and age is assigned an integer (30).

2. **Data Types**:
   - Python has several built-in data types, each serving different purposes:
     - **Integers** (int): Whole numbers, e.g., 10, -3.
     - **Floats** (float): Decimal numbers, e.g., 3.14, -0.5.
     - **Strings** (str): Text, enclosed in single or double quotes, e.g., "Hello", 'Python'.
     - **Booleans** (bool): Represent True or False values, used in logical operations.
   - You can check a variable's data type with type(), e.g.:

```python
Copy code
print(type(age))  # Output: <class 'int'>
```

3. **Basic Operators**:
   - **Arithmetic Operators**: Used for mathematical calculations:

```python
Copy code
x = 10
y = 3
print(x + y)   # Addition, Output: 13
print(x - y)   # Subtraction, Output: 7
print(x * y)   # Multiplication, Output: 30
print(x / y)   # Division, Output: 3.333...
print(x % y)   # Modulus (remainder), Output: 1
print(x ** y)  # Exponentiation, Output: 1000
```

○ **Comparison Operators**: Used to compare values, resulting in True or False:

```python
Copy code
print(x > y)   # Output: True
print(x == y)  # Output: False
```

○ **Logical Operators**: Used for combining conditions:

```python
Copy code
is_sunny = True
is_weekend = False
print(is_sunny and is_weekend)  # Output: False
print(is_sunny or is_weekend)   # Output: True
```

```
print(not is_sunny)        # Output: False
```

Control Structures: Loops and Conditionals

Control structures allow you to create programs that make decisions and perform repetitive tasks.

1. **Conditionals (if, elif, else)**:
   - Conditionals allow your program to make decisions based on certain conditions.
   - The basic syntax is:

     ```python
     Copy code
     temperature = 25
     if temperature > 30:
         print("It's a hot day!")
     elif temperature < 15:
         print("It's a cold day!")
     else:
         print("It's a pleasant day!")
     ```

   - Here, the code will print a message based on the value of temperature.

2. **Loops**:
   - Loops let you repeat a block of code multiple times. Python has two main types of loops: for and while.
   - **For Loop**:

- Used to iterate over a sequence (like a list or range of numbers):

python
Copy code

```
for i in range(1, 6):  # Iterates from 1 to 5
    print(i)        # Output: 1 2 3 4 5
```

- You can also iterate through elements in a list:

python
Copy code

```
fruits = ["apple", "banana", "cherry"]
for fruit in fruits:
    print(fruit)
```

o **While Loop**:
- Repeats as long as a specified condition is true:

python
Copy code

```
count = 0
while count < 5:
    print(count)
```

```
    count += 1    # Increments count to avoid an
infinite loop
```

Working with Functions and Creating Reusable Code

Functions are blocks of reusable code that allow you to break down your program into manageable parts.

1. **Defining Functions**:
   o Functions are defined using the def keyword, followed by the function name and parameters (if any):

   ```python
   Copy code
   def greet(name):
       print("Hello, " + name + "!")
   ```

   o You can call this function by passing in a value for name:

   ```python
   Copy code
   greet("Alice")  # Output: Hello, Alice!
   ```

2. **Return Values**:

o   Functions can return values using the return keyword. This allows you to store the function's output in a variable:

```python
Copy code
def add(a, b):
    return a + b
result = add(3, 4)
print(result)  # Output: 7
```

3. **Default Parameters**:

   o   You can set default parameter values, making them optional when calling the function:

```python
Copy code
def greet(name="stranger"):
    print("Hello, " + name + "!")
greet()         # Output: Hello, stranger!
greet("Alice")  # Output: Hello, Alice!
```

4. **Benefits of Functions**:

   o   Functions help organize code, make it reusable, and reduce repetition. They're particularly useful when you need to perform the same task multiple times in different parts of a program.

Example Project: Writing a Simple Calculator

Let's apply what we've learned so far by creating a simple calculator that performs basic operations based on user input.

1. **Define the Calculator Functions**:

    o Start by defining functions for addition, subtraction, multiplication, and division:

    python
    Copy code

    ```python
    def add(x, y):
        return x + y


    def subtract(x, y):
        return x - y


    def multiply(x, y):
        return x * y


    def divide(x, y):
        if y != 0:
            return x / y
        else:
            return "Error! Division by zero."
    ```

2. **Setting Up the Calculator Logic**:

o Use a loop to repeatedly prompt the user for input and perform the selected operation.

o Add conditionals to check the operation chosen by the user and call the appropriate function:

python
Copy code

```python
def calculator():
    print("Select operation:")
    print("1. Add")
    print("2. Subtract")
    print("3. Multiply")
    print("4. Divide")

    while True:
        choice = input("Enter choice (1/2/3/4) or 'q' to quit: ")

        if choice == 'q':
            print("Exiting calculator.")
            break

        if choice in ('1', '2', '3', '4'):
            num1 = float(input("Enter first number: "))
            num2 = float(input("Enter second number: "))
```

```python
        if choice == '1':
            print("Result:", add(num1, num2))
        elif choice == '2':
            print("Result:", subtract(num1, num2))
        elif choice == '3':
            print("Result:", multiply(num1, num2))
        elif choice == '4':
            print("Result:", divide(num1, num2))
    else:
        print("Invalid input, please try again.")
```

3. **Running the Calculator**:

   o Save this code in a file called calculator.py and run it by typing:

   bash
   Copy code
   python calculator.py

   o The calculator will prompt you to enter an operation and two numbers. It will display the result and prompt again until you decide to quit by entering 'q'.

In this chapter, you've learned essential Python syntax and concepts, including variables, data types, operators, control structures, and functions. These are the foundational tools you'll use to build more complex programs and automate tasks effectively. By creating a simple calculator program, you've also gained hands-on experience with structuring a small project using these concepts.

With these basics under your belt, you're ready to start exploring how to automate specific tasks using Python, starting with file and folder operations in the next chapter.

CHAPTER 3: AUTOMATING SIMPLE TASKS WITH PYTHON

Python's versatility shines in its ability to automate tedious, repetitive tasks, allowing you to focus on more important work. This chapter introduces automation concepts, explains Python's role in simplifying tasks, and demonstrates how to automate basic calculations and file operations. By the end, you'll create a practical script to automatically organize files in folders.

Overview of Automation and Python's Role

Automation is the process of using technology to perform tasks with minimal human intervention. By automating repetitive tasks, we save time, reduce errors, and streamline workflows. Python is ideal for automation because of its easy-to-read syntax and extensive library support.

Here are some typical tasks that Python can automate:

- Repetitive calculations

- File management (copying, renaming, deleting)
- Data entry and processing
- Web scraping and interacting with web services
- Sending automated emails or messages

Python's simplicity allows you to write automation scripts quickly, while libraries like **os** (for file operations), **shutil** (for file management), and **math** (for calculations) make complex tasks easier.

Automating Repetitive Math Calculations

Let's start with automating math calculations. Python's built-in functions and libraries handle calculations efficiently, reducing the need for repetitive work.

1. **Using Basic Math Functions**:
   - Python's math module offers various functions for common mathematical operations.
   - For example, if you frequently calculate areas of circles, you could automate this task.

python
Copy code

```
import math

def calculate_circle_area(radius):
    return math.pi * (radius ** 2)
```

```
radii = [2, 5, 7.5, 10]
for r in radii:
    print(f"Area of circle with radius {r}: {calculate_circle_area(r)}")
```

2. **Automating Complex Calculations**:
   - Suppose you need to perform a series of calculations on a list of values, like converting temperatures.
   - Python's functions and loops allow you to automate repetitive calculations efficiently.

python

Copy code

```
def celsius_to_fahrenheit(celsius):
    return (celsius * 9/5) + 32


temperatures = [0, 20, 37, 100]
for temp in temperatures:
    print(f"{temp}°C is {celsius_to_fahrenheit(temp)}°F")
```

Automating Basic File Operations (Copying, Renaming, Deleting)
Python's **os** and **shutil** modules provide tools for automating file and folder operations, allowing you to manage files programmatically.

1. **Copying Files**:
   o The shutil.copy() function copies a file from one location to another.
   o Example: Copy a file named report.txt from the current directory to a backup folder.

python
Copy code
import shutil

shutil.copy("report.txt", "backup/report_backup.txt")

2. **Renaming Files**:
   o The os.rename() function allows you to rename files. This is useful when organizing or updating filenames in bulk.
   o Example: Renaming old_document.txt to new_document.txt.

python
Copy code
import os

os.rename("old_document.txt", "new_document.txt")

3. **Deleting Files**:

- o You can use os.remove() to delete a file or shutil.rmtree() to delete an entire directory.
- o Example: Delete a temporary file or clear a temp folder.

python
Copy code

```
import os
import shutil

# Deleting a single file
os.remove("temp_file.txt")

# Deleting an entire directory
shutil.rmtree("temp_folder")
```

4. **Listing Files in a Directory**:
   - o os.listdir() lists all files and folders in a directory, which is useful for automation scripts that need to process files in bulk.
   - o Example: List all files in the documents folder.

python
Copy code

```
import os
```

```
files = os.listdir("documents")
for file in files:
    print(file)
```

Practical Example: Script to Organize Files in Folders

Now, let's combine these operations to create a useful automation script. We'll build a script that organizes files in a folder by file type, such as moving all .jpg files into an Images folder and all .txt files into a Text folder.

1. **Plan the Script**:
   o Our script will:
      ▪ Create folders based on file types if they don't exist.
      ▪ Move each file into the corresponding folder.
2. **Create the Script**:
   o Open your code editor and create a new file called organize_files.py.

```python
Copy code
import os
import shutil


# Directory to organize
```

```python
directory = "Downloads"

# Define folders for each file type
file_types = {
    "Images": [".jpg", ".jpeg", ".png", ".gif"],
    "Documents": [".pdf", ".docx", ".txt"],
    "Spreadsheets": [".xlsx", ".csv"],
    "Videos": [".mp4", ".mov", ".avi"]
}

# Create folders for each file type if they don't exist
for folder in file_types.keys():
    folder_path = os.path.join(directory, folder)
    if not os.path.exists(folder_path):
        os.makedirs(folder_path)

# Organize files into folders
for filename in os.listdir(directory):
    file_path = os.path.join(directory, filename)

    # Skip if it's a folder
    if os.path.isdir(file_path):
        continue

    # Move files to appropriate folders based on extension
```

```
for folder, extensions in file_types.items():
    if any(filename.lower().endswith(ext) for ext in extensions):
        shutil.move(file_path, os.path.join(directory, folder, filename))
        print(f"Moved {filename} to {folder} folder")
        break
```

3. **Explanation of the Script**:
   o **Folder Creation**: For each file type, the script checks if the folder exists. If not, it creates the folder using os.makedirs().
   o **File Sorting**: The script iterates through all files in the directory. For each file, it checks its extension and moves it to the corresponding folder using shutil.move().

4. **Running the Script**:
   o Save your script and run it in the command line:

   bash
   Copy code
   python organize_files.py

   o If the script is set to organize files in the Downloads folder, you should see each file moved into a folder based on its type.

5. **Customizing the Script**:

   o You can easily expand this script by adding more file types, changing the target directory, or logging each operation to a file for reference.

In this chapter, you learned about the basics of automation with Python. You explored how to automate repetitive math calculations and manipulate files with common operations like copying, renaming, and deleting. Using these skills, you created a practical script to organize files by type, which is a powerful example of how Python can save time and reduce manual work.

Now that you have a foundation in simple automation tasks, you're ready to tackle more specialized automation in the next chapters, starting with handling text data and performing more complex file manipulations.

CHAPTER 4: WORKING WITH STRINGS AND TEXT MANIPULATION

Text manipulation is a common task in automation, whether it's formatting messages, processing data, or generating dynamic content. In this chapter, we'll dive into Python's string-handling capabilities, covering basic operations like searching, replacing, and formatting text. By the end, you'll apply these concepts to create an automation script for email templates and responses, a valuable tool for handling repetitive communication.

Manipulating Text Data with Python

Python makes working with strings easy and intuitive, offering a variety of methods for manipulating text data. Strings are sequences of characters enclosed in single (' ') or double (" ") quotes. You can access individual characters, slice substrings, and use built-in methods to perform a wide range of operations.

1. **Basic String Operations**:
   - **Concatenation**: Combining strings with the + operator.

   python
   Copy code

```
greeting = "Hello, " + "world!"
print(greeting)  # Output: Hello, world!
```

- o **Repeating Strings**: Multiplying strings by an integer.

```python
Copy code
separator = "=" * 10
print(separator)  # Output: ==========
```

2. **String Indexing and Slicing**:
    - o **Indexing** allows you to access specific characters in a string.

```python
Copy code
text = "Python"
print(text[0])   # Output: P
print(text[-1])  # Output: n
```

- o **Slicing** allows you to extract substrings.

```python
Copy code
print(text[1:4]) # Output: yth
print(text[:3])  # Output: Pyt
```

```python
print(text[3:])   # Output: hon
```

3. **Common String Methods**:

   o **len()**: Returns the length of a string.

   o **upper() / lower()**: Converts to uppercase or lowercase.

   python
   Copy code
   ```python
   print("hello".upper())  # Output: HELLO
   ```

   o **strip()**: Removes whitespace from the beginning and end of a string.

   python
   Copy code
   ```python
   text = "   spaced out   "
   print(text.strip())  # Output: spaced out
   ```

   o **replace(old, new)**: Replaces occurrences of old with new.

   python
   Copy code
   ```python
   message = "I love apples."
   print(message.replace("apples", "bananas"))   # Output: I love bananas.
   ```

Common String Operations: Search, Replace, and Format

1. **Searching in Strings**:
   - Python provides several ways to search for substrings.
   - **in Operator**: Checks if a substring exists within a string.

     python
     Copy code
     ```
     phrase = "The quick brown fox"
     print("quick" in phrase)  # Output: True
     ```

   - **find() and index()**: Returns the position of the substring's first occurrence.

     python
     Copy code
     ```
     print(phrase.find("brown"))  # Output: 10
     ```

2. **Replacing Text**:
   - **replace(old, new)** replaces all instances of a substring with another string.
   - This method is especially useful for dynamic content generation or text transformations.
   - Example:

```python
Copy code
sentence = "Welcome to New York"
sentence = sentence.replace("New York", "Los Angeles")
print(sentence)  # Output: Welcome to Los Angeles
```

3. **String Formatting**:

   o Formatting strings is essential for creating dynamic messages and templates. Python provides several ways to format strings, including f-strings, format(), and the % operator.

   o **f-strings**: Introduced in Python 3.6, f-strings are one of the easiest ways to format strings.

```python
Copy code
name = "Alice"
age = 25
print(f"Hello, {name}. You are {age} years old.")  # Output: Hello, Alice. You are 25 years old.
```

   o **format() Method**: Useful for more complex formatting.

```python
Copy code
```

```
template = "The price of {item} is ${price:.2f}"
print(template.format(item="apple", price=1.5))   #
Output: The price of apple is $1.50
```

Practical Example: Automating Email Templates and Responses

Automating email templates is a common and highly useful task, particularly in business environments. In this example, we'll create a script that dynamically fills in an email template based on user data.

1. **Define the Email Template**:
   o Let's start by creating a simple email template with placeholders for name, date, and specific content.
   o Here's an example template:

   python
   Copy code
   ```
   email_template = """
   Hi {name},
   ```

   Thank you for reaching out on {date}. We have reviewed your request and are happy to assist you.

   Please let us know if you need further help.

   Best regards,

The Customer Support Team
"""

2. **Create the Automation Script**:
    o   We'll create a function to fill in the placeholders with dynamic values, then simulate sending an email by printing it to the console.

python
Copy code

```python
from datetime import date

# Function to generate personalized email
def generate_email(name, custom_content):
    today = date.today().strftime("%B %d, %Y")
    email_template = """
Hi {name},

Thank you for reaching out on {date}. {content}

Please let us know if you need further help.

Best regards,
The Customer Support Team
"""
```

```
    email = email_template.format(name=name, date=today,
content=custom_content)
    return email


# Sample data for demonstration
customer_data = [
    {"name": "Alice", "custom_content": "We have updated
your profile information as requested."},
    {"name": "Bob", "custom_content": "Your order has
been shipped and will arrive soon."},
]


# Generate and display personalized emails
for customer in customer_data:
    email        =        generate_email(customer["name"],
customer["custom_content"])
    print("Sending email...\n")
    print(email)
    print("="*50)
```

3. **Explanation of the Script**:
    o **Template Creation**: The email_template variable includes placeholders {name}, {date}, and {content} to be filled dynamically.
    o **Function to Generate Email**: The generate_email function takes the recipient's name and custom

content, retrieves today's date, and formats the email by filling in the placeholders.

- ○ **Loop through Customer Data**: For each customer in the sample data list, the script generates a personalized email message and prints it to simulate sending.

4. **Running the Script**:

- ○ Save this code in a file, such as email_automation.py, and run it:

```bash
Copy code
python email_automation.py
```

- ○ The output should look something like this:

```csharp
Copy code
Sending email...
```

Hi Alice,

Thank you for reaching out on March 15, 2023. We have updated your profile information as requested.

Please let us know if you need further help.

Best regards,

The Customer Support Team

Sending email...

Hi Bob,

Thank you for reaching out on March 15, 2023. Your order has been shipped and will arrive soon.

Please let us know if you need further help.

Best regards,

The Customer Support Team

5. **Further Enhancements**:

   o **Reading Data from a File**: You can enhance this script to read customer data from a CSV file or a database, making it more scalable.

   o **Automated Email Sending**: To actually send these emails, you could integrate this script with Python's smtplib library or an email API.

In this chapter, you explored the basics of string manipulation in Python, including common operations like searching, replacing, and formatting text. These skills are essential for working with text-based data and generating dynamic content, especially in automation tasks. The example of creating automated email templates and responses illustrates how Python can streamline repetitive communication, saving time and reducing errors.

In the next chapter, we'll build on these text manipulation skills by exploring how to work with files and folders in greater depth, preparing for automation tasks involving data storage and retrieval.

CHAPTER 5: WORKING WITH LISTS, DICTIONARIES, AND SETS

Python's built-in data structures—lists, dictionaries, and sets—are essential tools for organizing, storing, and processing collections of data. In this chapter, we'll explore how to use these data structures effectively, from creating and modifying collections to looping through and applying changes. By the end, you'll build a practical example of managing a list of contacts or inventory items.

Organizing Data with Lists, Dictionaries, and Sets

1. **Lists**:
   - **Definition**: Lists are ordered, mutable collections that allow duplicate items. They're ideal for storing sequences of data, like names or item quantities.
   - **Creating a List**:

     python
     Copy code
     ```
     fruits = ["apple", "banana", "cherry"]
     ```

   - **Accessing Items**:

- Use indices to access items, with indexing starting from 0.

python

Copy code

```python
print(fruits[0])  # Output: apple
print(fruits[-1]) # Output: cherry (last item)
```

- **Adding/Removing Items**:
    - append() adds an item, remove() deletes a specific item, and pop() removes an item by index.

python

Copy code

```python
fruits.append("orange")
fruits.remove("banana")
fruits.pop(0)  # Removes "apple"
```

2. **Dictionaries**:
    - **Definition**: Dictionaries store key-value pairs, allowing quick lookup of data based on keys. They're useful for structured data, like mapping names to phone numbers.
    - **Creating a Dictionary**:

python

```
Copy code
contact_info = {
    "Alice": "alice@example.com",
    "Bob": "bob@example.com"
}
```

- **Accessing and Modifying Values**:
  - Access values by key, and use square brackets to update existing entries.

```python
python
Copy code
print(contact_info["Alice"])        #    Output:
alice@example.com
contact_info["Alice"] = "alice_new@example.com"
```

- **Adding and Removing Entries**:
  - Add new key-value pairs directly and remove items with del.

```python
python
Copy code
contact_info["Charlie"] = "charlie@example.com"
del contact_info["Bob"]
```

3. **Sets**:

- **Definition**: Sets are unordered collections of unique items, which makes them ideal for eliminating duplicates or performing set operations like union and intersection.

- **Creating a Set**:

python
Copy code
```
unique_numbers = {1, 2, 3, 4}
```

- **Adding and Removing Items**:
  - Use add() to add and remove() to delete items.

python
Copy code
```
unique_numbers.add(5)
unique_numbers.remove(2)
```

- **Set Operations**:
  - Sets support operations like union (|), intersection (&), and difference (-).

python
Copy code
```
set_a = {1, 2, 3}
set_b = {3, 4, 5}
```

```
print(set_a | set_b)  # Union: {1, 2, 3, 4, 5}
print(set_a & set_b)  # Intersection: {3}
```

Looping Through and Modifying Data Collections

1. **Looping Through Lists**:
   - You can iterate through a list using a for loop.

   python
   Copy code
   ```
   fruits = ["apple", "banana", "cherry"]
   for fruit in fruits:
       print(fruit)
   ```

2. **Looping Through Dictionaries**:
   - Use .items() to get both keys and values in each iteration.

   python
   Copy code
   ```
   contact_info = {"Alice": "alice@example.com", "Bob": "bob@example.com"}
   for name, email in contact_info.items():
       print(f"{name}: {email}")
   ```

3. **Looping Through Sets**:

  o   Sets are unordered, but you can still iterate through them.

python

Copy code

```
unique_numbers = {1, 2, 3}
for number in unique_numbers:
   print(number)
```

4. **Modifying Collections in Place**:

  o   When modifying lists, dictionaries, or sets during iteration, take care to avoid changing the collection's size directly. Use list comprehension or a temporary list if necessary.

  o   **Example**: Removing items conditionally.

python

Copy code

```
numbers = [1, 2, 3, 4, 5]
numbers = [num for num in numbers if num > 2]  #
Keeps only numbers greater than 2
```

Real-World Example: Managing a List of Contacts or Inventory Items

In this example, we'll create a program to manage a list of contacts, allowing you to add, view, update, and delete contacts. Each contact will have a name, phone number, and email.

1. **Plan the Data Structure**:
   - We'll use a **list of dictionaries**, where each dictionary represents a contact with name, phone, and email keys.

python

Copy code

```
contacts = [
    {"name": "Alice", "phone": "123-456-7890", "email": "alice@example.com"},
    {"name": "Bob", "phone": "987-654-3210", "email": "bob@example.com"}
]
```

2. **Define Functions for Each Operation**:
   - We'll create functions to add a contact, view all contacts, update a contact's details, and delete a contact.

3. **Writing the Functions**:

python

Copy code

```
# Function to add a new contact
```

```python
def add_contact(contacts, name, phone, email):
    contacts.append({"name": name, "phone": phone,
"email": email})
    print(f"Added {name} to contacts.")


# Function to view all contacts
def view_contacts(contacts):
    for contact in contacts:
        print(f"Name: {contact['name']}, Phone:
{contact['phone']}, Email: {contact['email']}")


# Function to update a contact
def update_contact(contacts, name, phone=None,
email=None):
    for contact in contacts:
        if contact["name"].lower() == name.lower():
            if phone:
                contact["phone"] = phone
            if email:
                contact["email"] = email
            print(f"Updated contact for {name}.")
            return
    print(f"Contact {name} not found.")


# Function to delete a contact
```

```python
def delete_contact(contacts, name):
    for i, contact in enumerate(contacts):
        if contact["name"].lower() == name.lower():
            del contacts[i]
            print(f"Deleted contact {name}.")
            return
    print(f"Contact {name} not found.")
```

4. **Putting It All Together**:
   - We'll write a simple menu system to call each function based on user input.

python

Copy code

```python
def main():
    contacts = [
        {"name": "Alice", "phone": "123-456-7890", "email": "alice@example.com"},
        {"name": "Bob", "phone": "987-654-3210", "email": "bob@example.com"}
    ]

    while True:
        print("\nContact Manager")
        print("1. View Contacts")
        print("2. Add Contact")
```

```python
        print("3. Update Contact")
        print("4. Delete Contact")
        print("5. Exit")

        choice = input("Enter your choice: ")

        if choice == '1':
            view_contacts(contacts)
        elif choice == '2':
            name = input("Enter name: ")
            phone = input("Enter phone: ")
            email = input("Enter email: ")
            add_contact(contacts, name, phone, email)
        elif choice == '3':
            name = input("Enter name of contact to update: ")
            phone = input("Enter new phone (or leave blank): ")
            email = input("Enter new email (or leave blank): ")
            update_contact(contacts, name, phone if phone else
None, email if email else None)
        elif choice == '4':
            name = input("Enter name of contact to delete: ")
            delete_contact(contacts, name)
        elif choice == '5':
            print("Exiting Contact Manager.")
            break
```

```
else:

    print("Invalid choice. Please try again.")


if __name__ == "__main__":
  main()
```

5. **Running the Program**:
    - Save the code in a file named contact_manager.py and run it:

      bash

      Copy code

      python contact_manager.py

    - You'll be prompted to enter choices for viewing, adding, updating, or deleting contacts. The program will update the contacts list accordingly and display relevant feedback.

6. **Further Enhancements**:
    - **Data Persistence**: You could save contacts to a file (like a JSON or CSV file) to preserve them between sessions.
    - **Search Functionality**: Add a search function to look up contacts by partial name or email.
    - **Sorting**: Sort contacts alphabetically when displaying them.

In this chapter, you've learned how to work with lists, dictionaries, and sets to organize data. You've seen how to loop through and modify these collections, and you applied these concepts to create a practical contact manager program. These skills are essential when dealing with structured data, enabling you to automate tasks like organizing contacts, managing inventory, or processing lists of records.

In the next chapter, we'll dive into working with CSV and Excel files, which are common formats for storing tabular data in many industries. You'll learn to read, write, and process these files to expand your automation capabilities.

CHAPTER 6: FILES AND FOLDERS AUTOMATION

Automating file and folder tasks can save hours of manual work. In this chapter, you'll learn how to read from and write to files, manage files and directories programmatically, and create an automated file backup and sorting system. By the end, you'll have the skills to build a script that organizes files, creates backups, and helps keep your data safe and organized.

Reading from and Writing to Files

Python's built-in functions make it simple to read from and write to files. Files are often used to store data, logs, and configuration settings, so automating file handling can streamline many tasks.

1. **Opening and Closing Files**:
   - Use Python's open() function to open files. Specify the mode, such as:
     - **'r' (read)**: Opens a file for reading (default mode).
     - **'w' (write)**: Opens a file for writing (overwrites existing content).

- **'a' (append)**: Opens a file for appending (adds content to the end).
  - It's best practice to use with to handle files, as it automatically closes the file when done:

python

Copy code

```
with open("example.txt", "r") as file:
    content = file.read()
```

2. **Reading from Files**:
   - **Reading Entire Content**: file.read() reads the entire file as a single string.
   - **Reading Line-by-Line**: file.readlines() reads all lines and returns them as a list of strings.

python

Copy code

```
with open("example.txt", "r") as file:
    for line in file:
        print(line.strip())    # .strip() removes any
trailing newline characters
```

3. **Writing to Files**:
   - **Write Mode ('w')**: Overwrites the file if it exists or creates a new file.

- o **Append Mode ('a')**: Adds new content to the end of an existing file.

python

Copy code

```
with open("example.txt", "w") as file:
    file.write("This is a new line of text.\n")
```

4. **Working with Different File Formats**:
   - o **CSV Files**: Use the csv module to handle comma-separated values.
   - o **JSON Files**: Use the json module to store data in JSON format.
   - o **Example for JSON**:

python

Copy code

```
import json

data = {"name": "Alice", "age": 25}
with open("data.json", "w") as file:
    json.dump(data, file)
```

Organizing Files and Directories Programmatically

Python's **os** and **shutil** modules allow you to manage files and folders programmatically, enabling you to create, move, delete, and organize files.

1. **Creating and Deleting Directories**:
   - **os.makedirs()**: Creates directories, including parent directories if they don't exist.
   - **os.rmdir()**: Deletes an empty directory. Use **shutil.rmtree()** to delete a directory with content.

python
Copy code
```
import os
import shutil

os.makedirs("backup_folder", exist_ok=True)   # Creates 'backup_folder' if it doesn't exist
shutil.rmtree("backup_folder")   # Deletes 'backup_folder' and its contents
```

2. **Moving and Copying Files**:
   - Use the **shutil** module to move and copy files easily.
   - **shutil.move()**: Moves a file from one directory to another.
   - **shutil.copy()**: Copies a file.

python

Copy code

```
shutil.move("example.txt", "backup/example.txt")  # Moves the file to the backup folder
shutil.copy("example.txt", "backup/example_backup.txt")  # Copies the file
```

3. **Renaming Files**:
   - **os.rename()**: Renames a file or directory.

python

Copy code

```
os.rename("old_file.txt", "new_file.txt")
```

4. **Listing Files in a Directory**:
   - **os.listdir()**: Returns a list of files and directories in the specified path.
   - **glob.glob()**: Use this to match files with specific patterns (e.g., *.txt for all text files).

python

Copy code

```
files = os.listdir("my_directory")
for file in files:
    print(file)
```

Example Project: Creating a File Backup and Sorting System

This project will help you create a system to automatically organize files by type, back up important files, and keep your directories neat and safe.

1. **Plan the Project**:
    - o We'll create a script that:
        - ▪ Backs up specified file types (e.g., .txt and .jpg) to a backup folder.
        - ▪ Sorts files into folders based on file type (e.g., all images go into an Images folder, documents go into a Documents folder).

2. **Set Up File and Folder Paths**:
    - o Define paths for the main directory (where files are located) and the backup directory.

```python
Copy code
import os
import shutil
from datetime import datetime

main_directory = "my_files"
backup_directory = "backup"
os.makedirs(backup_directory, exist_ok=True)
```

3. **Define File Categories**:

- o Create a dictionary to map file types to specific folders.

python
Copy code

```python
file_categories = {
    "Images": [".jpg", ".jpeg", ".png", ".gif"],
    "Documents": [".pdf", ".docx", ".txt"],
    "Spreadsheets": [".xlsx", ".csv"],
    "Videos": [".mp4", ".mov", ".avi"]
}
```

4. **Backup and Sort Files**:
   - o Write the script to iterate through files in the main directory, back them up to the backup folder, and then move them to the appropriate category folder.

python
Copy code

```python
def backup_and_sort_files():
    # Create timestamp for backup folder
    timestamp = datetime.now().strftime("%Y%m%d_%H%M%S")
    backup_folder = os.path.join(backup_directory, f"backup_{timestamp}")
    os.makedirs(backup_folder, exist_ok=True)
```

```python
    # Iterate through files in main directory
    for filename in os.listdir(main_directory):
        file_path = os.path.join(main_directory, filename)

        # Skip if it's a directory
        if os.path.isdir(file_path):
            continue

        # Backup the file
        shutil.copy(file_path, backup_folder)
        print(f"Backed up {filename} to {backup_folder}")

        # Sort the file by category
        file_ext = os.path.splitext(filename)[1].lower()    # Extract file extension
        moved = False
        for category, extensions in file_categories.items():
            if file_ext in extensions:
                category_folder = os.path.join(main_directory, category)
                os.makedirs(category_folder, exist_ok=True)
                shutil.move(file_path, os.path.join(category_folder, filename))
                print(f"Moved {filename} to {category} folder")
```

```
            moved = True
            break


    # If file doesn't match any category, move to "Others"
folder
    if not moved:
        others_folder    =    os.path.join(main_directory,
"Others")
        os.makedirs(others_folder, exist_ok=True)
        shutil.move(file_path,    os.path.join(others_folder,
filename))
        print(f"Moved {filename} to Others folder")


# Run the function
backup_and_sort_files()
```

5. **Explanation of the Script**:
   - **Backup with Timestamps**: Each backup run creates a new folder in backup_directory with a timestamp, ensuring that previous backups are not overwritten.
   - **File Sorting**: Files are sorted into folders by file extension. If a file doesn't match any predefined category, it goes into an "Others" folder.

○ **Directory Creation**: Folders for each file category and backups are created only if they don't already exist.

6. **Running the Script**:

○ Save the code as file_manager.py and run it:

bash

Copy code

python file_manager.py

○ The script will create a timestamped backup folder, copy files into it, and sort the files in the main directory.

Further Enhancements

1. **Logging**:

○ Add logging to track which files were moved, backed up, or encountered errors.

python

Copy code

import logging

logging.basicConfig(filename="file_manager.log", level=logging.INFO)

logging.info("Script run completed")

2. **Automated Scheduling**:

   o Use a task scheduler (e.g., cron on Linux, Task Scheduler on Windows) to run the script periodically and keep files organized automatically.

3. **Email Notification**:

   o Consider adding email notifications after each run, summarizing the backup and organization process.

In this chapter, you've learned to automate file and folder tasks using Python. You practiced reading from and writing to files, managing directories, and created an automated system to back up and organize files by type. These skills are foundational for maintaining organized data and ensuring important files are safely backed up.

In the next chapter, we'll expand on data automation by working with CSV and Excel files, commonly used in data analysis and record-keeping.

CHAPTER 7: WORKING WITH CSV AND EXCEL FILES

CSV (Comma-Separated Values) and Excel files are widely used for storing tabular data, especially in business, finance, and research. In this chapter, you'll learn how to automate tasks like reading and writing to CSV files, manipulating Excel spreadsheets using Python's **openpyxl** library, and working with structured data efficiently. By the end, we'll apply these skills to a practical example: automating data entry and updating records in an Excel file.

eading from and Writing to CSV Files

CSV files are text files where data is separated by commas, making them easy to read, edit, and process. Python's built-in **csv** module provides functions for handling these files.

1. **Reading CSV Files**:
    o **csv.reader**: Use this function to read CSV files row-by-row.

o **Example**: Suppose we have a students.csv file with the following content:

css
Copy code
```
name,age,grade
Alice,14,A
Bob,15,B
Charlie,13,A
```

o Here's how to read this data:

python
Copy code
```
import csv

with open("students.csv", mode="r") as file:
    csv_reader = csv.reader(file)
    for row in csv_reader:
        print(row)
```

o Output:

css
Copy code
```
['name', 'age', 'grade']
['Alice', '14', 'A']
```

['Bob', '15', 'B']

['Charlie', '13', 'A']

2. **Writing to CSV Files**:

   o **csv.writer**: This function writes data to CSV files.

   o **Example**: Writing a list of records to a new CSV file.

   python
   Copy code

```python
data = [
    ["name", "age", "grade"],
    ["Alice", 14, "A"],
    ["Bob", 15, "B"],
    ["Charlie", 13, "A"]
]

with open("new_students.csv", mode="w", newline="") as file:
    csv_writer = csv.writer(file)
    csv_writer.writerows(data)
```

   o This will create a new file, new_students.csv, with the same content.

3. **Using csv.DictReader and csv.DictWriter**:

- These classes allow you to work with rows as dictionaries, using column headers as keys.
- **Example**: Reading the students.csv file with DictReader.

python
Copy code

```
with open("students.csv", mode="r") as file:
    csv_reader = csv.DictReader(file)
    for row in csv_reader:
        print(f"{row['name']} is {row['age']} years old and got grade {row['grade']}.")
```

4. **Appending to a CSV File**:
   - Use mode="a" to append new data without overwriting existing content.
   - **Example**: Adding a new record to students.csv.

python
Copy code

```
new_student = ["David", 16, "B"]

with open("students.csv", mode="a", newline="") as file:
    csv_writer = csv.writer(file)
    csv_writer.writerow(new_student)
```

Automating Basic Excel Tasks Using openpyxl

The **openpyxl** library allows you to automate Excel tasks, such as creating spreadsheets, updating cells, and managing sheets. Install openpyxl using pip if you haven't done so already:

bash

Copy code

```
pip install openpyxl
```

1. **Creating and Saving Excel Workbooks**:
   o To create a new workbook and add data:

   python

   Copy code

   ```
   from openpyxl import Workbook

   workbook = Workbook()
   sheet = workbook.active
   sheet.title = "Students"

   # Adding headers
   sheet.append(["Name", "Age", "Grade"])

   # Adding data
   sheet.append(["Alice", 14, "A"])
   ```

```python
sheet.append(["Bob", 15, "B"])

# Save the workbook
workbook.save("students.xlsx")
```

2. **Reading Data from Excel Files**:
   - **openpyxl.load_workbook** loads an existing Excel file, and you can specify a sheet to read data from.

   python
   Copy code
   ```python
   from openpyxl import load_workbook

   workbook = load_workbook("students.xlsx")
   sheet = workbook["Students"]

   for row in sheet.iter_rows(values_only=True):
       print(row)
   ```

3. **Updating Cells and Writing Data**:
   - Access cells by their coordinates (like A1, B2) to update values.

   python
   Copy code
   ```python
   sheet["B2"] = 16  # Updates Bob's age to 16
   workbook.save("students.xlsx")
   ```

4. **Adding Formulas**:

   o Excel formulas can be added as string values in cells. They will calculate when the file is opened in Excel.

   python
   Copy code

```python
sheet["C4"] = "=AVERAGE(B2:B3)"  # Calculates average age of Alice and Bob
workbook.save("students.xlsx")
```

5. **Conditional Formatting**:

   o Apply conditional formatting to cells to highlight values based on conditions. Here's an example highlighting cells with an "A" grade.

   python
   Copy code

```python
from openpyxl.styles import PatternFill

for row in sheet.iter_rows(min_row=2, max_row=sheet.max_row, min_col=3, max_col=3):
    for cell in row:
        if cell.value == "A":
            cell.fill = PatternFill(start_color="FFFF00", end_color="FFFF00", fill_type="solid")
```

```
workbook.save("students.xlsx")
```

Practical Example: Automating Data Entry and Updating Records in Excel

Let's create a script to automate data entry and update records in an Excel file. This example is useful for maintaining an inventory or contact list.

1. **Scenario**:
   - You have an Excel file called inventory.xlsx with columns for **Item Name**, **Quantity**, and **Price**.
   - You need a script to:
     - Add new items.
     - Update quantities for existing items.
     - Calculate the total inventory value.

2. **Setup**:
   - Here's a sample structure for inventory.xlsx:

     css
     Copy code

Item Name	Quantity	Price
Widget A	10	2.50
Widget B	5	3.75

3. **Writing the Script**:

```python
Copy code
from openpyxl import load_workbook, Workbook

# Load or create workbook and sheet
try:
    workbook = load_workbook("inventory.xlsx")
    sheet = workbook.active
except FileNotFoundError:
    workbook = Workbook()
    sheet = workbook.active
    sheet.title = "Inventory"
    sheet.append(["Item Name", "Quantity", "Price"])  # Headers
    workbook.save("inventory.xlsx")


def add_or_update_item(item_name, quantity, price):
    # Check if item already exists and update quantity if so
    for row in sheet.iter_rows(min_row=2, values_only=False):
        if row[0].value == item_name:
            row[1].value += quantity
            print(f"Updated {item_name} quantity to {row[1].value}.")
            workbook.save("inventory.xlsx")
```

```python
        return

        # If item does not exist, add it
        sheet.append([item_name, quantity, price])
        print(f"Added new item: {item_name}, Quantity: {quantity}, Price: {price}.")
        workbook.save("inventory.xlsx")

def calculate_total_inventory_value():
    total_value = 0
    for row in sheet.iter_rows(min_row=2, values_only=True):
        item_value = row[1] * row[2]  # Quantity * Price
        total_value += item_value
    return total_value

# Add or update items
add_or_update_item("Widget A", 5, 2.50)
add_or_update_item("Widget C", 10, 4.00)

# Calculate and display total inventory value
total_value = calculate_total_inventory_value()
print(f"Total inventory value: ${total_value:.2f}")
```

4. **Explanation of the Script**:

- o **Load or Create Workbook**: The script tries to load inventory.xlsx. If the file doesn't exist, it creates a new workbook and adds headers.
- o **add_or_update_item**: This function checks if an item already exists. If it does, it updates the quantity. Otherwise, it adds a new row with the item details.
- o **calculate_total_inventory_value**: This function calculates the total value by iterating over all rows and multiplying each item's quantity by its price.

5. **Running the Script**:
- o Save the code as inventory_manager.py and run it:

bash

Copy code

python inventory_manager.py

- o The script will update the Excel file based on the items specified in the function calls and display the total inventory value.

6. **Further Enhancements**:
- o **User Input**: Extend the script to take item details from user input.
- o **Data Validation**: Add checks to validate quantities and prices.
- o **Automated Reports**: Use this script as a base to create automated reports in Excel.

In this chapter, you learned to work with CSV and Excel files to automate data entry and record management. Python's **csv** module makes handling CSV files straightforward, while **openpyxl** provides powerful tools for Excel automation, including reading, writing, formatting, and applying formulas. The practical example of an inventory management script illustrates how to use these skills for real-world automation tasks.

In the next chapter, we'll explore web scraping with Python, enabling you to collect data from websites and integrate it into your automated workflows.

CHAPTER 8: AUTOMATING WEB SCRAPING WITH PYTHON

Web scraping is a powerful technique for collecting data from websites automatically. With web scraping, you can gather information such as prices, product details, or weather forecasts to use in your projects. In this chapter, we'll cover the basics of web scraping, introduce two essential Python libraries—**requests** and **BeautifulSoup**—and provide an example project to scrape and save data from a website.

Introduction to Web Scraping and Legal Considerations

1. **What is Web Scraping?**
   - o Web scraping is the process of extracting data from websites programmatically. Rather than manually copying information, you can use a script to gather data from multiple pages and store it for analysis, reports, or automation tasks.

2. **Applications of Web Scraping**:
   - o Collecting product prices for price comparison.

- o Aggregating news articles or blog posts.

- o Monitoring weather data or stock prices.

- o Gathering data for research or data science projects.

3. **Legal Considerations**:

   - o **Terms of Service**: Always review a website's Terms of Service to ensure that scraping is permitted. Many websites prohibit scraping in their terms, and ignoring these rules can result in your IP being banned or legal action.

   - o **Robots.txt**: Most websites have a robots.txt file, which specifies which parts of the site are off-limits to web crawlers. You can find this file by appending /robots.txt to the website's domain (e.g., https://example.com/robots.txt). Respect the guidelines in this file.

   - o **API Alternatives**: If a website offers an API, it's often preferable to use the API rather than scraping HTML pages, as APIs are designed for data access and often provide structured, reliable data.

Using Libraries like BeautifulSoup and requests

To scrape data from websites, we'll use two popular Python libraries:

- • **requests**: For sending HTTP requests to websites and retrieving their content.

- **BeautifulSoup**: For parsing HTML and navigating through the page structure to extract specific data.

1. **Installing Required Libraries**:
   - Install requests and BeautifulSoup using pip:

   bash
   Copy code
   pip install requests beautifulsoup4

2. **Using requests to Fetch Web Content**:
   - The requests library allows you to fetch the HTML content of a webpage.
   - **Example**: Fetching a webpage using requests.get():

   python
   Copy code
   import requests

   url = "https://example.com"
   response = requests.get(url)

   # Check if request was successful
   if response.status_code == 200:
       print("Page retrieved successfully!")
       print(response.text) # Prints the HTML content of the page

else:

```
print(f"Failed       to      retrieve      page:
{response.status_code}")
```

3. **Parsing HTML with BeautifulSoup**:

   o BeautifulSoup helps you navigate and search through HTML content.

   o **Example**: Creating a BeautifulSoup object and printing the page title.

   python
   Copy code

```python
from bs4 import BeautifulSoup

# Initialize BeautifulSoup with the HTML content
soup = BeautifulSoup(response.text, "html.parser")

# Get the title of the page
print("Page Title:", soup.title.string)
```

4. **Finding HTML Elements**:

   o BeautifulSoup provides various methods to locate elements by tags, classes, and IDs:

      ▪ **find()**: Finds the first occurrence of a tag.

      ▪ **find_all()**: Finds all occurrences of a tag.

- **CSS Selectors**: Use .select() for CSS-style selectors.
  - **Example**: Finding all links on a page:

```python
Copy code
links = soup.find_all("a")
for link in links:
    print(link.get("href"))  # Prints the URL in each
<a> tag's href attribute
```

Example Project: Scraping and Saving Data from a Website
In this project, we'll create a script to scrape product data from a fictional e-commerce page and save it to a CSV file. This example will demonstrate practical web scraping skills, including fetching content, parsing HTML, and organizing data for storage.

1. **Project Overview**:
   - We'll scrape product names, prices, and availability status from a sample webpage (e.g., https://example.com/products).
   - The data will be saved to a CSV file named products.csv.
2. **Fetching the Webpage Content**:
   - Start by requesting the webpage and checking the response.

```python
Copy code
import requests

url = "https://example.com/products"
response = requests.get(url)

if response.status_code == 200:
    print("Page retrieved successfully!")
else:
    print("Failed to retrieve the page.")
```

3. **Parsing the HTML and Extracting Data**:

   o Next, initialize BeautifulSoup and locate elements with product details. Let's assume each product is contained within a <div> with a class of "product-item".

```python
Copy code
from bs4 import BeautifulSoup

# Parse the HTML content
soup = BeautifulSoup(response.text, "html.parser")

# Find all product containers
```

```python
products = soup.find_all("div", class_="product-item")

# Extract data for each product
product_data = []
for product in products:
    name = product.find("h2", class_="product-name").text.strip()
    price = product.find("span", class_="product-price").text.strip()
    availability = product.find("span", class_="availability-status").text.strip()

    # Add to the product data list
    product_data.append({
        "name": name,
        "price": price,
        "availability": availability
    })
```

4. **Saving Data to a CSV File**:
   o Using the **csv** module, we can save the scraped data in a structured format.

python
Copy code
import csv

```python
# Define the headers
headers = ["name", "price", "availability"]

# Write data to CSV
with open("products.csv", mode="w", newline="") as file:
    writer = csv.DictWriter(file, fieldnames=headers)
    writer.writeheader()  # Write the header row
    writer.writerows(product_data)  # Write product rows

print("Data saved to products.csv")
```

5. **Running the Script**:

   o Save the code as scrape_products.py and run it:

   bash

   Copy code

   python scrape_products.py

   o After running, a file named products.csv should be created with rows containing product names, prices, and availability statuses.

6. **Sample CSV Output**:

   o The generated products.csv file might look like this:

   mathematica

   Copy code

name,price,availability

Product A,$19.99,In Stock

Product B,$29.99,Out of Stock

Product C,$15.99,In Stock

Handling Common Web Scraping Challenges

1. **Dynamic Content (JavaScript-Rendered Pages)**:
   - Some pages load content dynamically via JavaScript, making them difficult to scrape with requests.
   - **Solution**: Use **Selenium** to automate a web browser and capture rendered content. Alternatively, check if the website provides an API.

2. **HTTP Errors and Status Codes**:
   - Always check the HTTP status code of a response. Common status codes include:
     - **200 OK**: The request was successful.
     - **404 Not Found**: The page doesn't exist.
     - **403 Forbidden**: Access is restricted (often requires login or authorization).
   - **Solution**: Implement error handling and consider including headers, such as User-Agent, to mimic a legitimate browser request.

3. **Delays and Rate Limiting**:

- o Websites may limit the frequency of requests to prevent scraping.
- o **Solution**: Add delays between requests using time.sleep() to avoid getting blocked.

4. **Captcha and Anti-Scraping Measures**:
   - o Some websites use captchas or other anti-scraping tools.
   - o **Solution**: Consider using a scraping API service, or in some cases, Selenium with captcha-solving services.

In this chapter, you learned the fundamentals of web scraping, including how to make requests to a website and use BeautifulSoup to parse HTML and extract data. We implemented an example project to scrape product information and save it to a CSV file, covering the entire process from fetching content to organizing data for storage. With these skills, you can automate data collection from websites and gather insights without manual data entry.

In the next chapter, we'll explore using APIs to access web data, which is often a more efficient and reliable method for gathering information from websites that provide structured data APIs.

CHAPTER 9: AUTOMATING BROWSER TASKS WITH SELENIUM

Selenium is a powerful tool that allows you to control a web browser programmatically. It's commonly used for automating web tasks like form submissions, button clicks, navigation, and even handling JavaScript-rendered content that can't be accessed through standard web scraping. In this chapter, we'll introduce Selenium, cover basic browser automation tasks, and walk through a real-world example of automating a login and data extraction process.

Overview of Selenium and Automating Browsers

1. **What is Selenium?**

   o Selenium is an open-source tool primarily used for testing web applications, but it's also popular for web automation. It allows you to control a browser (like Chrome or Firefox) using Python code, mimicking the actions of a real user.

2. **Why Use Selenium?**

   o Selenium is useful when:

      ▪ A website's content is loaded dynamically via JavaScript (which isn't accessible through traditional web scraping methods).

      ▪ You need to interact with web elements (e.g., filling out forms, clicking buttons).

      ▪ A website requires user actions like login before data is accessible.

3. **Setting Up Selenium**:

   o To use Selenium, you need:

      ▪ **Selenium Python library**: Install via pip.

      ▪ **WebDriver**: A driver specific to the browser you want to automate, like ChromeDriver for Chrome or GeckoDriver for Firefox.

   o **Installing Selenium**:

   bash

   Copy code

   pip install selenium

   o **Download the WebDriver**:

- ChromeDriver: https://sites.google.com/a/chromium.org/chromedriver/downloads
- GeckoDriver for Firefox: https://github.com/mozilla/geckodriver/releases

  o **Starting the Browser**:
  - Place the downloaded driver in a directory included in your PATH, or specify its path directly.
  - **Example**: Starting Chrome with Selenium.

```python
Copy code
from selenium import webdriver


driver = webdriver.Chrome()   # Or specify path: webdriver.Chrome(executable_path='path/to/chromedriver')
driver.get("https://example.com")
```

Filling Out Forms, Clicking Buttons, and Navigation

Selenium provides a range of methods to interact with web elements. Let's explore how to find elements, fill out forms, click buttons, and navigate through pages.

1. **Finding Elements**:
   - Selenium offers several methods for locating elements:
     - **find_element_by_id**: Finds an element by its id attribute.
     - **find_element_by_name**: Finds an element by its name attribute.
     - **find_element_by_class_name**: Finds an element by its CSS class.
     - **find_element_by_xpath**: Finds an element using an XPath expression.
   - **Example**: Finding elements on a page.

   python
   Copy code

   ```python
   search_box = driver.find_element_by_name("q")  # Find search box by name
   login_button = driver.find_element_by_id("login")  # Find login button by ID
   ```

2. **Filling Out Forms**:
   - To fill out a form, find the input field and use the send_keys() method to enter text.
   - **Example**: Filling out a search box.

   python

Copy code

```
search_box = driver.find_element_by_name("q")
search_box.send_keys("Selenium automation")
```

3. **Clicking Buttons**:
   - Locate the button element and use click() to simulate a click.
   - **Example**: Clicking a login button.

   python
   Copy code

   ```
   login_button = driver.find_element_by_id("login-button")
   login_button.click()
   ```

4. **Navigating Between Pages**:
   - Selenium allows you to navigate to URLs or move forward and backward in the browser's history.
   - **Example**: Navigating to a new page.

   python
   Copy code

   ```
   driver.get("https://example.com/dashboard")
   ```

5. **Waiting for Elements to Load**:
   - Sometimes elements take time to load, especially on JavaScript-heavy sites. Selenium's WebDriverWait

allows you to wait until an element becomes available.

- o **Example**: Waiting for an element to be clickable.

python
Copy code

```python
from selenium.webdriver.common.by import By
from selenium.webdriver.support.ui import WebDriverWait
from selenium.webdriver.support import expected_conditions as EC

# Wait until the login button is clickable, up to 10 seconds
login_button = WebDriverWait(driver, 10).until(
    EC.element_to_be_clickable((By.ID, "login-button"))
)
login_button.click()
```

Real-World Example: Automating Login and Data Extraction

In this example, we'll automate logging into a website, navigating to a specific section, and extracting data. Let's assume we have an account on a mock website with data available only after logging in.

1. **Project Overview**:
   - Goal: Log into https://example.com with a username and password, then extract specific data from the dashboard (e.g., recent transactions).
   - Process:
     - Open the login page.
     - Enter the username and password.
     - Click the login button.
     - Navigate to the dashboard and extract transaction data.

2. **Setting Up**:
   - Define the URL, username, and password (for this example, we'll use placeholder values).
   - Define paths to each element using id, name, or XPath selectors.

3. **Writing the Script**:

```python
Copy code
from selenium import webdriver
from selenium.webdriver.common.by import By
from selenium.webdriver.support.ui import WebDriverWait
from selenium.webdriver.support import expected_conditions as EC
import time
```

```python
# Define login credentials and URL
url = "https://example.com/login"
username = "your_username"
password = "your_password"

# Start the WebDriver and open the login page
driver = webdriver.Chrome()
driver.get(url)

# Log in to the site
try:
    # Enter username
    username_input = WebDriverWait(driver, 10).until(
        EC.presence_of_element_located((By.ID,
"username"))
    )
    username_input.send_keys(username)

    # Enter password
    password_input                                    =
driver.find_element_by_id("password")
    password_input.send_keys(password)

    # Click the login button
```

```
    login_button      =      driver.find_element_by_id("login-
button")
    login_button.click()

    # Wait until the dashboard loads
    WebDriverWait(driver, 10).until(

EC.presence_of_element_located((By.CLASS_NAME,
"dashboard"))
    )
    print("Logged in successfully!")

except Exception as e:
    print("Error during login:", e)
    driver.quit()

# Navigate to the dashboard and extract data
try:
    # Find the transactions section
    transactions                                =
driver.find_elements_by_class_name("transaction-item")

    # Extract and print transaction details
    for transaction in transactions:
```

```
        date                                        =
transaction.find_element_by_class_name("transaction-
date").text
        amount                                      =
transaction.find_element_by_class_name("transaction-
amount").text
        description                                 =
transaction.find_element_by_class_name("transaction-
description").text
        print(f"Date: {date}, Amount: {amount}, Description:
{description}")


except Exception as e:
    print("Error during data extraction:", e)


# Close the browser
finally:
    driver.quit()
```

4. **Explanation of the Script**:
   - **Login Process**: The script waits for the username and password fields to load, enters the credentials, and clicks the login button.
   - **Waiting for Elements**: Using WebDriverWait, we ensure elements like the login button and dashboard load fully before interacting with them.

- ○ **Data Extraction**: After logging in, the script looks for elements with class "transaction-item" to get transaction details like date, amount, and description. Each piece of data is printed to the console.

5. **Running the Script**:

   - ○ Save the code as automate_login.py and run it:

   bash

   Copy code

   ```
   python automate_login.py
   ```

   - ○ The script should log into the website, navigate to the dashboard, extract transaction data, and print it to the console.

6. **Example Output**:

   yaml

   Copy code

   ```
   Logged in successfully!
   Date: 2023-03-01, Amount: $150.00, Description: Grocery Store
   Date: 2023-03-02, Amount: $50.00, Description: Gas Station
   Date: 2023-03-03, Amount: $200.00, Description: Electronics Store
   ```

Tips for Handling Common Issues with Selenium Automation

1. **Dynamic Content and Loading Delays**:
   - Use WebDriverWait to wait for elements that load slowly or are dynamically rendered.

2. **Error Handling**:
   - Wrap actions in try-except blocks to handle errors gracefully and provide meaningful messages.

3. **Headless Mode**:
   - If you don't need to see the browser, you can run it in headless mode for faster execution:

   ```python
   Copy code
   options = webdriver.ChromeOptions()
   options.add_argument("--headless")
   driver = webdriver.Chrome(options=options)
   ```

4. **Browser Window Management**:
   - Control window size or maximize the browser window for elements that depend on screen resolution:

   ```python
   Copy code
   ```

driver.maximize_window()

In this chapter, you learned to automate browser tasks with Selenium, covering basic interactions like filling forms, clicking buttons, and navigating pages. We created a real-world example to automate a login and extract data from a website's dashboard. Selenium's ability to handle dynamic content and simulate user interactions makes it an excellent tool for automating web tasks that are otherwise difficult to access.

In the next chapter, we'll dive into working with APIs to access web data programmatically, providing a more direct and efficient approach for data extraction when a website offers an API.

CHAPTER 10: WORKING WITH APIS FOR AUTOMATION

APIs (Application Programming Interfaces) provide a structured way to interact with data and services offered by websites and online platforms. APIs allow you to retrieve data in a machine-readable format (typically JSON), making them an ideal tool for automation. In this chapter, you'll learn the basics of working with APIs, how to make requests and handle responses, and implement a project that uses a weather API to get daily forecasts.

Understanding APIs and JSON Data

1. **What is an API?**
    - An API (Application Programming Interface) is a set of rules and protocols that enables two applications to communicate with each other. APIs often allow applications to request data or perform actions on a server.

o Many websites and online services (like Twitter, Google, and weather sites) provide APIs to access their data programmatically.

2. **RESTful APIs**:

o REST (Representational State Transfer) is a popular architectural style for APIs. RESTful APIs typically use HTTP requests like **GET** (to retrieve data) and **POST** (to send data) to interact with resources.

o REST APIs usually return data in **JSON** (JavaScript Object Notation) format, which is easy to parse and work with in Python.

3. **Understanding JSON**:

o JSON is a lightweight data format that is human-readable and structured as key-value pairs.

o **Example JSON** data:

json
Copy code
```
{
  "location": "New York",
  "forecast": [
    {"day": "Monday", "temperature": 22, "condition": "Sunny"},
    {"day": "Tuesday", "temperature": 18, "condition": "Rainy"}
  ]
```

```
}
```

- In Python, JSON data can be represented as a dictionary or a list of dictionaries, making it easy to access specific values.

Making API Requests and Handling Responses

Python's **requests** library is ideal for making HTTP requests to APIs, handling responses, and parsing JSON data. Let's explore the basics of making an API request and working with the response.

1. **Installing the Requests Library**:
   - If you haven't already, install requests using pip:

   bash

   Copy code

   pip install requests

2. **Making a GET Request**:
   - A **GET** request is used to retrieve data from an API endpoint.
   - **Example**: Making a request to a mock weather API endpoint.

   python

   Copy code

   import requests

```
url = "https://api.example.com/weather"
response = requests.get(url)

# Check if the request was successful
if response.status_code == 200:
    print("Data retrieved successfully!")
    print(response.text)    # Print the raw JSON
response
else:
    print(f"Failed        to        retrieve        data:
{response.status_code}")
```

3. **Parsing JSON Responses**:
   o Use the json() method to parse JSON data directly into a Python dictionary.
   o **Example**: Accessing JSON data from the response.

   python
   Copy code
   ```
   if response.status_code == 200:
       data = response.json()    # Convert JSON to a
   dictionary
       print("Location:", data["location"])
       print("Forecast        for        Monday:",
   data["forecast"][0])
   ```

4. **Handling API Authentication**:

   o Some APIs require an **API key** for access. This key is usually provided in the request headers or as a URL parameter.

   o **Example**: Adding an API key to the request.

   python
   Copy code

   ```python
   api_key = "your_api_key"
   url = f"https://api.example.com/weather?apikey={api_key}"
   response = requests.get(url)
   ```

5. **Error Handling**:

   o Implement error handling to deal with potential issues like invalid requests or network errors.

   o **Example**: Basic error handling for common HTTP status codes.

   python
   Copy code

   ```python
   if response.status_code == 200:
       data = response.json()
   elif response.status_code == 404:
       print("Data not found.")
   ```

```
else:
    print("An error occurred:", response.status_code)
```

Example Project: Using a Weather API to Get Daily Forecasts

In this project, we'll build a script to retrieve daily weather forecasts from an online weather API and print the forecast for each day. We'll use OpenWeatherMap's API for this example, which provides weather information for cities worldwide. You'll need to sign up for an API key on OpenWeatherMap's website to access their data.

1. **Project Setup**:
   - Sign up on OpenWeatherMap and get an API key.
   - Define the base URL and city for which you want the weather forecast.
2. **Writing the Script**:

   python
   Copy code
   ```python
   import requests
   from datetime import datetime

   # Define API key, base URL, and parameters
   api_key = "your_openweathermap_api_key"
   base_url = "https://api.openweathermap.org/data/2.5/forecast"
   ```

```python
city = "New York"

# Make the API request
params = {
    "q": city,
    "appid": api_key,
    "units": "metric"  # Use "imperial" for Fahrenheit
}
response = requests.get(base_url, params=params)

# Check if the request was successful
if response.status_code == 200:
    data = response.json()
    print(f"Weather forecast for {city}:\n")

    # Extract and display the forecast data
    for forecast in data["list"]:
        timestamp = forecast["dt"]
        date = datetime.fromtimestamp(timestamp).strftime("%Y-%m-%d %H:%M:%S")
        temperature = forecast["main"]["temp"]
        condition = forecast["weather"][0]["description"]

        print(f"Date: {date}")
```

```python
    print(f"Temperature: {temperature}°C")
    print(f"Condition: {condition.capitalize()}\n")
else:
    print("Failed to retrieve data:", response.status_code)
```

3. **Explanation of the Script**:
    - ○ **API Request**: We set parameters like the city name, API key, and units of measurement. We use requests.get() to make the API call.
    - ○ **Parsing and Displaying Data**: The response JSON contains forecast data in a list under data["list"]. For each forecast, we extract the timestamp, temperature, and weather condition, then format the date and print the data.

4. **Running the Script**:
    - ○ Save the code as weather_forecast.py and run it:

    bash

    Copy code

    python weather_forecast.py

5. **Sample Output**:

    yaml

    Copy code

    Weather forecast for New York:

Date: 2023-11-01 09:00:00

Temperature: 15.3°C

Condition: Clear sky

Date: 2023-11-01 12:00:00

Temperature: 16.8°C

Condition: Few clouds

Date: 2023-11-01 15:00:00

Temperature: 17.2°C

Condition: Broken clouds

6. **Further Enhancements**:

   o **Save Data to a CSV File**: Use the csv module to save the forecast to a file for later analysis.

   o **Add Error Handling for API Limits**: Some APIs have rate limits (maximum requests per minute or day). Implement a pause (e.g., time.sleep()) if needed to avoid exceeding limits.

Tips for Working with APIs

1. **API Documentation**:

   o Always refer to the API documentation for details on endpoints, parameters, and response formats.

Documentation will also indicate if there are limits on the number of requests.

2. **API Key Security**:
   - o Never share your API key publicly. Consider storing it in environment variables or a configuration file.

3. **Handling Rate Limits**:
   - o Most APIs enforce rate limits to prevent abuse. Respect these limits by implementing pauses if necessary, or explore paid options if available.

4. **Testing and Debugging**:
   - o Use tools like Postman or curl to test API requests before coding them. These tools help you verify endpoints, parameters, and expected responses.

In this chapter, you learned the fundamentals of working with APIs, including making requests, handling JSON responses, and authenticating with an API key. Using a weather API, we created a practical project to fetch daily forecasts for a specified city, providing insight into how APIs can automate data retrieval. APIs are an essential tool for automating data gathering from web services, especially when websites provide APIs specifically designed for developers.

In the next chapter, we'll explore automating email and text messaging, enabling you to send notifications, alerts, or reminders directly from your scripts.

CHAPTER 11: AUTOMATING EMAIL AND TEXT MESSAGING

Automating emails and text messages can save time, streamline communications, and ensure timely reminders or alerts. This chapter will guide you through sending automated emails with Python's smtplib, using Twilio for sending text messages, and creating a real-world application that sends automated reminders or notifications.

Sending Automated Emails with smtplib

Python's built-in smtplib module allows you to send emails through an SMTP (Simple Mail Transfer Protocol) server. This approach works well for sending automated messages, notifications, and even reports.

1. **Understanding SMTP**:

- o SMTP servers handle email delivery. Many email providers, like Gmail, provide free SMTP servers for sending emails.
- o **Note**: Some providers (e.g., Gmail) require additional setup to allow SMTP access.

2. **Setting Up smtplib for Sending Emails**:
   - o To send an email, you'll need the SMTP server's details (e.g., host and port), the sender's email address, and a password or app-specific password for authentication.

3. **Writing the Script to Send an Email**:
   - o **Example**: Sending an email using Gmail's SMTP server.

```python
Copy code
import smtplib
from email.mime.text import MIMEText
from email.mime.multipart import MIMEMultipart

# Define the SMTP server and login credentials
smtp_server = "smtp.gmail.com"
smtp_port = 587
sender_email = "your_email@gmail.com"
password = "your_password"  # Use an app-specific password if required
```

```python
# Define the recipient and email content
recipient_email = "recipient@example.com"
subject = "Automated Notification"
body = """
Hello,

This is an automated notification sent from Python.

Best regards,
Your Automation Script
"""

# Create the email message
message = MIMEMultipart()
message["From"] = sender_email
message["To"] = recipient_email
message["Subject"] = subject
message.attach(MIMEText(body, "plain"))

# Send the email
try:
    with smtplib.SMTP(smtp_server, smtp_port) as server:
        server.starttls()  # Secure the connection
```

```
server.login(sender_email, password)
server.sendmail(sender_email, recipient_email,
message.as_string())
print("Email sent successfully!")
except Exception as e:
print("Error sending email:", e)
```

4. **Explanation of the Script**:
   - **Creating the Email**: We use MIMEMultipart to build the email, setting the sender, recipient, subject, and body.
   - **Connecting to the SMTP Server**: The script connects to the Gmail SMTP server with TLS encryption, logs in, and sends the email.
   - **Error Handling**: If there's an issue (e.g., incorrect login details), the script catches the exception and prints an error message.

5. **Using App-Specific Passwords**:
   - If you're using Gmail, you may need to create an app-specific password for added security. This can be generated from your Google account's security settings.

Sending Text Messages with Twilio or Similar Services

For sending text messages programmatically, we can use Twilio, a cloud communications platform that offers a simple API for SMS.

To get started, you'll need to create a Twilio account, set up a phone number, and obtain your account SID and auth token.

1. **Setting Up Twilio**:
   - Sign up on Twilio's website, create a project, and get your **account SID**, **auth token**, and **Twilio phone number**.
   - Install Twilio's Python package:

   bash
   Copy code
   ```
   pip install twilio
   ```

2. **Writing the Script to Send a Text Message**:
   - **Example**: Sending a text message using Twilio's API.

   python
   Copy code
   ```python
   from twilio.rest import Client

   # Twilio account credentials
   account_sid = "your_account_sid"
   auth_token = "your_auth_token"
   twilio_number = "your_twilio_phone_number"
   recipient_number = "+1234567890"   # Recipient's phone number
   ```

```
# Initialize the Twilio client
client = Client(account_sid, auth_token)

# Send the message
try:
    message = client.messages.create(
        body="Hello! This is an automated message from Python.",
        from_=twilio_number,
        to=recipient_number
    )
    print("Message sent successfully:", message.sid)
except Exception as e:
    print("Error sending message:", e)
```

3. **Explanation of the Script**:

   o **Authentication**: The Client class initializes with your Twilio account SID and auth token.

   o **Creating and Sending the Message**: The create method sends a text message with the specified body, sender's number, and recipient's number.

   o **Handling Errors**: If Twilio encounters an issue (e.g., invalid credentials), the script catches the exception and prints an error message.

4. **Additional Twilio Features**:

- o Twilio allows you to check the message's status, schedule messages, and even send multimedia messages (MMS) with images.

Real-World Application: Automated Reminders or Notifications

Let's create a practical application that sends reminders or notifications to users via email and text. This could be useful for appointment reminders, daily alerts, or task reminders.

1. **Project Overview**:
   - o We'll build a script that reads a list of reminders from a CSV file, then sends an email or text message to each user with their personalized reminder.
2. **Sample CSV File (reminders.csv)**:
   - o Create a CSV file with columns for **name**, **contact_type** (email or SMS), **contact** (email address or phone number), and **message**.
   - o Example:

   kotlin
   Copy code

   ```
   name,contact_type,contact,message
   Alice,email,alice@example.com,Your appointment
   is tomorrow at 3 PM.
   ```

Bob,sms,+1234567890,Don't forget to submit your report today.

3. **Writing the Script**:

```python
Copy code
import csv
import smtplib
from email.mime.text import MIMEText
from email.mime.multipart import MIMEMultipart
from twilio.rest import Client

# Email configuration
smtp_server = "smtp.gmail.com"
smtp_port = 587
sender_email = "your_email@gmail.com"
email_password = "your_password"

# Twilio configuration
account_sid = "your_account_sid"
auth_token = "your_auth_token"
twilio_number = "your_twilio_phone_number"

# Initialize the Twilio client
client = Client(account_sid, auth_token)
```

```python
def send_email(recipient, subject, body):
    message = MIMEMultipart()
    message["From"] = sender_email
    message["To"] = recipient
    message["Subject"] = subject
    message.attach(MIMEText(body, "plain"))

    try:
        with smtplib.SMTP(smtp_server, smtp_port) as server:
            server.starttls()
            server.login(sender_email, email_password)
            server.sendmail(sender_email, recipient, message.as_string())
        print(f"Email sent to {recipient}")
    except Exception as e:
        print(f"Failed to send email to {recipient}: {e}")

def send_sms(recipient, body):
    try:
        message = client.messages.create(
            body=body,
            from_=twilio_number,
            to=recipient
```

```
    )
    print(f"SMS sent to {recipient}: {message.sid}")
except Exception as e:
    print(f"Failed to send SMS to {recipient}: {e}")


# Reading reminders from the CSV file
with open("reminders.csv", mode="r") as file:
    csv_reader = csv.DictReader(file)
    for row in csv_reader:
        name = row["name"]
        contact_type = row["contact_type"]
        contact = row["contact"]
        message = row["message"]


        # Sending the reminder
        if contact_type == "email":
            subject = f"Reminder for {name}"
            send_email(contact, subject, message)
        elif contact_type == "sms":
            send_sms(contact, message)
```

4. **Explanation of the Script**:
   o **Reading from CSV**: The script reads each row from reminders.csv to get details like the user's name, contact type, contact info, and message.

- o **Sending Emails and Texts**: Based on the contact type, the script calls send_email for email reminders and send_sms for SMS reminders.
- o **Error Handling**: The script prints an error message if there's an issue sending a message.

5. **Running the Script**:
   - o Save the code as reminder_sender.py and run it:

   bash

   Copy code

   python reminder_sender.py

6. **Output**:
   - o The script will print success messages as it sends reminders, or display any errors encountered.

Further Enhancements

1. **Scheduling Reminders**:
   - o Use a scheduler like cron (Linux) or Task Scheduler (Windows) to run the script at specific times, such as daily or weekly.

2. **User-Friendly Message Templates**:
   - o Use placeholders in the messages (e.g., {name}) to create personalized reminders dynamically.

3. **Log Message Status**:

o Add logging to record when each message is sent successfully or when an error occurs. This can be useful for auditing and troubleshooting.

4. **Tracking Responses**:

o Twilio provides status tracking for SMS messages, allowing you to see if the message was delivered, read, or failed.

In this chapter, you learned how to automate sending emails with smtplib and text messages with Twilio. Using these tools, we built a practical application to send automated reminders or notifications. Automating communication tasks like reminders can save time, improve reliability, and ensure timely messaging.

In the next chapter, we'll dive into scheduling and timing techniques in Python, enabling you to set up automated tasks at specific times or intervals, which is useful for regular notifications, data scraping, and more.

CHAPTER 12: SCHEDULING AND TIMING WITH PYTHON

Automating tasks at specific times or intervals can save time and ensure that essential tasks are performed consistently. Python offers various tools for time-based automation, from basic scheduling with the time module to more advanced scheduling with the schedule library. In this chapter, you'll learn how to use these libraries to run tasks at regular intervals, and we'll walk through an example of automating a daily backup task.

Using Time-Based Automation with time and schedule Libraries

1. **Introduction to the time Module**:
   o The time module provides basic time-related functions, such as delaying execution (sleep()) and getting the current time. Although limited in

scheduling features, it's useful for adding delays and performing tasks at short intervals.

- o **Example**: Delay execution by 10 seconds.

```python
Copy code
import time


print("Starting task...")
time.sleep(10)  # Waits for 10 seconds
print("Task completed.")
```

2. **The schedule Library**:
   - o The schedule library is a simple but powerful tool for running tasks at specific intervals, like every hour, day, or week. This library makes it easy to set up recurring jobs without manually managing time calculations.
   - o **Installing schedule**:

```bash
Copy code
pip install schedule
```

   - o **Basic Usage**:
     - ▪ Define a function to run at specific intervals and register it with the scheduler.

- Use schedule.run_pending() in a loop to check and execute any due tasks.

```python
Copy code
import schedule
import time

def my_task():
    print("Running scheduled task...")

# Schedule the task every 5 seconds
schedule.every(5).seconds.do(my_task)

# Keep the script running to check for scheduled tasks
while True:
    schedule.run_pending()   # Run any pending scheduled tasks
    time.sleep(1)   # Wait for 1 second before checking again
```

3. **Scheduling Intervals with schedule**:
   o schedule supports various time intervals, such as:
      - schedule.every(10).seconds: Runs a task every 10 seconds.

- schedule.every().hour: Runs a task every hour.
- schedule.every().day.at("10:30"): Runs a task daily at 10:30 AM.
- schedule.every().monday: Runs a task every Monday.
  - **Example**: Running a task every day at a specific time.

python
Copy code

```python
def daily_task():
    print("Running daily task...")


schedule.every().day.at("09:00").do(daily_task)


while True:
    schedule.run_pending()
    time.sleep(1)
```

Automating Tasks at Regular Intervals

Automating tasks at regular intervals is useful for data backups, data collection, periodic notifications, and more. By combining Python's schedule library with custom functions, you can create scripts that run consistently and automatically.

1. **Setting Up Recurring Jobs**:
   - Define your task as a function.
   - Schedule the function to run at a regular interval, such as daily or weekly.

2. **Combining Multiple Tasks**:
   - You can use schedule to handle multiple jobs with different intervals. Simply add each task to the schedule, and schedule.run_pending() will manage them.
   - **Example**: Running different tasks at varying intervals.

   python
   Copy code
   ```python
   def task_one():
       print("Task one running every minute...")


   def task_two():
       print("Task two running every day at 8:00
   AM...")


   # Schedule tasks
   schedule.every(1).minutes.do(task_one)
   schedule.every().day.at("08:00").do(task_two)


   # Main loop to run scheduled tasks
   ```

```python
while True:
    schedule.run_pending()
    time.sleep(1)
```

Example: Automating a Daily Backup Task

In this example, we'll automate a daily backup process. Our script will back up files from a specified directory to a backup folder every day at a specific time.

1. **Project Overview**:
   o Define a source directory containing files to back up.
   o Set up a destination directory (backup folder).
   o Automate the backup task to run daily.

2. **Writing the Backup Script**:

```python
python
Copy code
import os
import shutil
from datetime import datetime
import schedule
import time

# Define source and backup directories
source_directory = "source_folder"
```

```python
backup_directory = "backup_folder"

# Create the backup folder if it doesn't exist
if not os.path.exists(backup_directory):
    os.makedirs(backup_directory)

def backup_files():
    # Create a timestamped folder in the backup directory
    timestamp                                    =
datetime.now().strftime("%Y%m%d_%H%M%S")
    backup_path       =       os.path.join(backup_directory,
f"backup_{timestamp}")
    os.makedirs(backup_path)

    # Copy files from source to backup folder
    for filename in os.listdir(source_directory):
        source_file = os.path.join(source_directory, filename)
        if os.path.isfile(source_file):
            shutil.copy2(source_file, backup_path)    # Copy
with metadata
            print(f"Backed up {filename} to {backup_path}")

    print(f"Backup completed at {timestamp}")

# Schedule the backup task to run daily at 2:00 AM
```

```
schedule.every().day.at("02:00").do(backup_files)
```

```
# Keep the script running
while True:
    schedule.run_pending()
    time.sleep(60)  # Check for scheduled tasks every minute
```

3. **Explanation of the Script**:
   - **Backup Function**: The backup_files() function creates a timestamped folder within the backup_directory and copies all files from the source_directory to this new folder.
   - **Scheduling the Backup**: We schedule backup_files() to run every day at 2:00 AM.
   - **Infinite Loop**: The script checks for scheduled tasks every minute. When the time reaches 2:00 AM, schedule.run_pending() will run backup_files().

4. **Running the Script**:
   - Save the code as daily_backup.py and run it:

     bash
     Copy code
     python daily_backup.py

   - The script will stay running, checking for the scheduled time. Each day at 2:00 AM, it will back

AUTOMATE THE BORING STUFF WITH PYTHON

up the files in the source_directory to a new folder in the backup_directory.

5. **Sample Output**:

bash

Copy code

Backed up document.txt to backup_folder/backup_20231108_020000

Backed up photo.jpg to backup_folder/backup_20231108_020000

Backup completed at 20231108_020000

Tips for Effective Time-Based Automation

1. **Run in the Background**:
   - o Use tools like nohup (Linux) or Task Scheduler (Windows) to run the script in the background, allowing it to execute even if the terminal is closed.

2. **Error Handling and Logging**:
   - o Add error handling and logging to your script for easier debugging and tracking of completed backups.
   - o **Example**: Log each backup task to a file.

   python

   Copy code

   import logging

```
logging.basicConfig(filename="backup_log.txt",
level=logging.INFO)

def backup_files():
    try:
        # Your backup code
        logging.info(f"Backup        completed        at
{datetime.now()}")
    except Exception as e:
        logging.error(f"Backup failed: {e}")
```

3. **Testing Your Scheduled Tasks**:
   o Before setting up a daily schedule, test your script with shorter intervals (e.g., every minute) to verify it works as expected.
   o **Example**: Use schedule.every(1).minutes.do(backup_files) for testing.

4. **Pausing and Stopping**:
   o If you need to pause or stop a scheduled task, comment out or remove the line where you schedule the task, or stop the script if it's running in the background.

5. **Using External Schedulers**:

o For more advanced scheduling (e.g., monthly or specific day-of-week combinations), consider using OS-level schedulers like **cron** (Linux/macOS) or **Task Scheduler** (Windows).

In this chapter, you learned how to automate tasks at specific intervals using Python's time module and the schedule library. We created a practical example of a daily backup script that runs automatically at a set time, ensuring that files are consistently backed up. Time-based automation can be applied to a wide variety of tasks, from data backups and reports to alerts and reminders.

In the next chapter, we'll explore working with PDFs and Word documents, enabling you to automate document creation, text extraction, and other file-based tasks.

CHAPTER 13: WORKING WITH PDFS AND WORD DOCUMENTS

Automating tasks with PDFs and Word documents can save significant time in generating, extracting, and managing reports and forms. In this chapter, you'll learn to read, write, and manipulate PDF files with the PyPDF2 library and automate Word documents with python-docx. We'll conclude with a practical example that automates report generation, a valuable skill in business and data-driven environments.

Reading, Writing, and Manipulating PDFs with PyPDF2

1. **Introduction to PyPDF2**:
   - PyPDF2 is a popular library for working with PDF files in Python. While it supports basic operations like reading, merging, and splitting PDFs, it doesn't

offer advanced editing (such as modifying text or images within a PDF).

- o Install PyPDF2 using pip:

bash

Copy code

pip install PyPDF2

2. **Reading PDF Content**:
   - o **Example**: Extracting text from a PDF file.

python

Copy code

```python
from PyPDF2 import PdfReader

# Open the PDF file
with open("example.pdf", "rb") as file:
    reader = PdfReader(file)
    num_pages = len(reader.pages)
    print(f"Number of pages: {num_pages}")

    # Extract text from each page
    for page_num in range(num_pages):
        page = reader.pages[page_num]
        text = page.extract_text()
        print(f"Page {page_num + 1}:\n{text}")
```

- o **Explanation**:
  - The script opens the PDF file, counts the pages, and extracts text from each page using extract_text(). Note that PyPDF2 may not perform perfectly with PDFs that contain images or scanned content.

3. **Writing (Merging) PDFs**:
   - o You can combine multiple PDF files into a single document using PdfWriter.
   - o **Example**: Merging two PDFs.

```python
Copy code
from PyPDF2 import PdfReader, PdfWriter

# Open the PDFs to merge
pdf1 = PdfReader(open("document1.pdf", "rb"))
pdf2 = PdfReader(open("document2.pdf", "rb"))
writer = PdfWriter()

# Add pages from the first PDF
for page in pdf1.pages:
    writer.add_page(page)

# Add pages from the second PDF
for page in pdf2.pages:
```

```python
    writer.add_page(page)

# Write the merged PDF to a new file
with open("merged_document.pdf", "wb") as output_file:
    writer.write(output_file)
print("PDFs merged successfully!")
```

4. **Extracting and Splitting Pages**:
   o **Example**: Extracting a specific page from a PDF.

   python
   Copy code
   ```python
   from PyPDF2 import PdfReader, PdfWriter

   # Open the source PDF and prepare the writer
   with open("example.pdf", "rb") as source_file:
       reader = PdfReader(source_file)
       writer = PdfWriter()

       # Extract a specific page (e.g., page 2)
       writer.add_page(reader.pages[1])  # Page indices start from 0

       # Write the extracted page to a new PDF
   ```

```
with    open("extracted_page.pdf",    "wb")    as
output_file:
    writer.write(output_file)
print("Page extracted successfully!")
```

Automating Word Documents with python-docx

python-docx is a library for creating, modifying, and reading Word (.docx) files. It allows you to automate tasks like generating reports, filling templates, and making edits to existing documents.

1. **Installing python-docx**:
   - Install python-docx using pip:

     bash

     Copy code

     pip install python-docx

2. **Creating a New Word Document**:
   - **Example**: Creating a simple Word document with headings, paragraphs, and bullet points.

     python

     Copy code

     from docx import Document

     # Create a new document
     doc = Document()

```python
# Add title and headings
doc.add_heading("Automated Report", level=1)
doc.add_paragraph("This is a report generated
automatically using Python.")


# Add a subheading and bullet points
doc.add_heading("Highlights", level=2)
highlights = ["Key finding 1", "Key finding 2",
"Key finding 3"]
for item in highlights:
    doc.add_paragraph(item, style="ListBullet")


# Save the document
doc.save("automated_report.docx")
print("Word document created successfully!")
```

3. **Modifying an Existing Word Document**:
   - You can open and edit an existing Word document by adding new paragraphs, updating text, or formatting content.
   - **Example**: Adding content to an existing document.

   python
   Copy code
   from docx import Document

```python
# Open an existing document
doc = Document("existing_report.docx")

# Add content to the document
doc.add_paragraph("New data has been added to this report.")

# Save the changes
doc.save("updated_report.docx")
print("Document updated successfully!")
```

4. **Using Tables in Word Documents**:
   - Tables are essential for presenting structured data in Word reports.
   - **Example**: Adding a table with data.

   python
   Copy code
   ```python
   from docx import Document

   doc = Document()
   doc.add_heading("Data Table", level=1)

   # Create a table with 3 rows and 3 columns
   table = doc.add_table(rows=3, cols=3)
   ```

```
data = [
    ["Header 1", "Header 2", "Header 3"],
    ["Row 1, Col 1", "Row 1, Col 2", "Row 1, Col 3"],
    ["Row 2, Col 1", "Row 2, Col 2", "Row 2, Col 3"]
]

for i, row_data in enumerate(data):
    row = table.rows[i]
    for j, cell_data in enumerate(row_data):
        row.cells[j].text = cell_data

# Save the document
doc.save("table_report.docx")
print("Word document with table created successfully!")
```

Practical Example: Automating Report Generation

In this example, we'll create an automated report in Word format. The report will contain a title, an introductory paragraph, a table with data, and some highlights in bullet points. This report could be generated daily, weekly, or on demand with updated data.

1. **Project Overview**:

  o Generate a report with a title, description, highlights, and a data table.

  o Save the report as a Word document.

2. **Writing the Report Generation Script**:

python

Copy code

```
from docx import Document
from datetime import datetime


def generate_report(data, highlights):
    # Create a new Word document
    doc = Document()


    # Add a title and introductory paragraph
    title = "Automated Report"
    doc.add_heading(title, level=1)
    doc.add_paragraph(f"Report generated on {datetime.now().strftime('%Y-%m-%d %H:%M:%S')}")
    doc.add_paragraph("This report was generated automatically and includes the latest data and insights.")


    # Add highlights as bullet points
    doc.add_heading("Highlights", level=2)
    for item in highlights:
        doc.add_paragraph(item, style="ListBullet")
```

```python
    # Add a data table
    doc.add_heading("Data Summary", level=2)
    table = doc.add_table(rows=1, cols=len(data[0]))

    # Add header row
    header_cells = table.rows[0].cells
    for i, header in enumerate(data[0]):
        header_cells[i].text = header

    # Add data rows
    for row_data in data[1:]:
        row = table.add_row().cells
        for j, cell_data in enumerate(row_data):
            row[j].text = str(cell_data)

    # Save the document
    filename                                        =
f"automated_report_{datetime.now().strftime('%Y%m%d')
}.docx"
    doc.save(filename)
    print(f"Report saved as {filename}")

# Example data
data = [
```

```
    ["Date", "Metric", "Value"],
    ["2023-11-01", "Metric A", "100"],
    ["2023-11-02", "Metric B", "200"],
    ["2023-11-03", "Metric C", "300"]
]
highlights = ["Increase in Metric A", "Steady growth in Metric B", "Metric C shows improvement"]


# Generate the report
generate_report(data, highlights)
```

3. **Explanation of the Script**:
    o **Title and Introductory Paragraph**: The script adds a title and a paragraph with the current date and time.
    o **Highlights**: Adds each highlight as a bullet point using the ListBullet style.
    o **Data Table**: Creates a table, adds headers from data[0], and populates each row with data.
    o **Saving the Report**: The report is saved with a filename that includes the current date.

4. **Running the Script**:
    o Save the code as generate_report.py and run it:

    bash
    Copy code

python generate_report.py

- o The script will create a Word document named automated_report_<date>.docx.

5. **Sample Output**:
   - o The generated Word document will contain the title, introductory paragraph, highlights as bullet points, and a data table with the provided data.

Further Enhancements

1. **Dynamic Data Sources**:
   - o Integrate with a database or API to pull real-time data for the report, such as sales data or performance metrics.
2. **Email Automation**:
   - o After generating the report, use Python's smtplib to email it as an attachment automatically.
3. **PDF Conversion**:
   - o Use a tool like reportlab or pdfkit to convert the Word report to a PDF automatically.
4. **Advanced Formatting**:
   - o Customize styles, fonts, and colors in python-docx for a more polished and branded report format.

In this chapter, you explored how to automate tasks with PDFs using PyPDF2 and Word documents with python-docx. These skills are valuable for generating, managing, and extracting information from documents, especially in environments where regular reporting is essential. The example project demonstrated how to automate report generation, a task that can save time and improve consistency in document creation.

In the next chapter, we'll look at image processing tasks in Python, focusing on resizing, cropping, and watermarking images to prepare them for various automated workflows.

CHAPTER 14: AUTOMATING IMAGE PROCESSING TASKS

Image processing tasks, like resizing, cropping, and watermarking, are essential for web development, digital marketing, and content creation. Python's **Pillow** library makes it easy to perform these tasks programmatically, automating repetitive image editing processes. In this chapter, we'll introduce the basics of image processing with Pillow, demonstrate how to resize, crop, and apply filters to images, and build a real-world example: an automated image watermarking tool.

Basics of Image Processing with PIL (Pillow)

Pillow (PIL) is a popular Python library for working with images. It provides functions for opening, manipulating, and saving images in various formats.

1. **Installing Pillow**:
   - Install Pillow using pip:

     bash
     Copy code
     pip install pillow

2. **Loading and Displaying an Image**:

- o Use Image.open() to load an image and .show() to display it.
- o **Example**: Opening and displaying an image.

python
Copy code
from PIL import Image

```
# Open an image file
image = Image.open("example.jpg")
image.show()   # Display the image in the default viewer
```

3. **Saving Images**:
   - o You can save images in different formats using the .save() method.
   - o **Example**: Saving an image as a PNG file.

python
Copy code
```
image.save("example_converted.png", format="PNG")
```

Resizing, Cropping, and Filtering Images

Pillow provides straightforward methods for resizing, cropping, and applying filters to images.

1. **Resizing Images**:
   - The .resize() method changes the dimensions of an image. You can specify new dimensions, and optionally, an interpolation method (e.g., Image.LANCZOS for high-quality resizing).
   - **Example**: Resizing an image to 800x800 pixels.

   ```python
   Copy code
   resized_image = image.resize((800, 800), Image.LANCZOS)
   resized_image.save("resized_example.jpg")
   ```

2. **Cropping Images**:
   - Cropping extracts a rectangular region from the image. Use .crop() with a bounding box (left, top, right, bottom).
   - **Example**: Cropping an image to a specific region.

   ```python
   Copy code
   cropped_image = image.crop((100, 100, 400, 400))
   # Crop region (left, top, right, bottom)
   cropped_image.save("cropped_example.jpg")
   ```

3. **Applying Filters**:

- Pillow's ImageFilter module provides several filters, like **BLUR, CONTOUR**, and **SHARPEN**.
- **Example**: Applying a blur filter to an image.

```python
Copy code
from PIL import ImageFilter

blurred_image = image.filter(ImageFilter.BLUR)
blurred_image.save("blurred_example.jpg")
```

4. **Rotating and Flipping Images**:
   - **Rotating**: Use .rotate() to rotate the image by a specific angle.
   - **Flipping**: Use .transpose() with Image.FLIP_LEFT_RIGHT or Image.FLIP_TOP_BOTTOM for horizontal or vertical flips.
   - **Example**: Rotating and flipping an image.

```python
Copy code
rotated_image = image.rotate(45)    # Rotate 45 degrees
```

```
flipped_image                          =
image.transpose(Image.FLIP_LEFT_RIGHT)      #
Flip horizontally
rotated_image.save("rotated_example.jpg")
flipped_image.save("flipped_example.jpg")
```

Real-World Example: Creating an Automated Image Watermarking Tool

Adding watermarks to images is a common task in content creation to protect intellectual property. In this example, we'll create a tool that automatically applies a watermark to images.

1. **Project Overview**:

   o The tool will load an image and a watermark, resize the watermark to fit, and place it in the bottom-right corner.

   o The watermark will have an adjustable transparency level, allowing you to control its visibility.

2. **Writing the Watermarking Script**:

   python
   Copy code

   ```python
   from PIL import Image, ImageEnhance
   ```

```python
def     apply_watermark(image_path,     watermark_path,
output_path, position="bottom-right", opacity=0.5):
    # Open the main image and watermark image
    image = Image.open(image_path).convert("RGBA")
    watermark                                    =
Image.open(watermark_path).convert("RGBA")

    # Resize watermark to 1/4 the width of the original
image
    width_ratio = image.width // 4
    watermark        =        watermark.resize((width_ratio,
int(width_ratio * watermark.height / watermark.width)))

    # Adjust watermark transparency
    watermark = adjust_opacity(watermark, opacity)

    # Calculate position for the watermark
    if position == "bottom-right":
        x = image.width - watermark.width - 10  # 10 pixels
padding
        y = image.height - watermark.height - 10
    elif position == "bottom-left":
        x = 10
        y = image.height - watermark.height - 10
    elif position == "top-right":
```

```
        x = image.width - watermark.width - 10
        y = 10
    elif position == "top-left":
        x = 10
        y = 10
    else:
        # Center position
        x = (image.width - watermark.width) // 2
        y = (image.height - watermark.height) // 2

    # Paste the watermark onto the image
    watermarked_image = Image.alpha_composite(image,
watermark_positioned(image, watermark, x, y))

    # Convert to RGB and save the final watermarked image
    watermarked_image.convert("RGB").save(output_path,
"JPEG")
    print(f"Watermarked image saved to {output_path}")


def adjust_opacity(watermark, opacity):
    """Adjusts the opacity of the watermark image."""
    alpha = watermark.split()[3]  # Extract the alpha channel
    alpha                                            =
ImageEnhance.Brightness(alpha).enhance(opacity)        #
Adjust opacity
```

```python
    watermark.putalpha(alpha)
    return watermark


def watermark_positioned(image, watermark, x, y):
    """Creates a new image with the watermark placed in the
specified position."""
    transparent_image = Image.new("RGBA", image.size)
    transparent_image.paste(watermark, (x, y), watermark)
    return transparent_image


# Applying the watermark
apply_watermark(
    image_path="input_image.jpg",
    watermark_path="watermark.png",
    output_path="watermarked_image.jpg",
    position="bottom-right",
    opacity=0.5
)
```

3. **Explanation of the Script**:
    - ○ **apply_watermark Function**: This function loads the main image and watermark, resizes the watermark to 1/4 of the image's width, adjusts its opacity, and positions it according to the specified location.

- o **Adjusting Opacity**: The adjust_opacity function modifies the watermark's transparency to make it less intrusive.
- o **Watermark Positioning**: Depending on the position parameter, the watermark is placed in one of the corners or in the center of the image.

4. **Running the Script**:
   - o Save the code as watermark_tool.py and run it:

   bash
   Copy code
   python watermark_tool.py

   - o The script will create a watermarked version of input_image.jpg and save it as watermarked_image.jpg.

5. **Sample Output**:
   - o The watermarked image will display the watermark at the specified position with the desired opacity.

Further Enhancements

1. **Batch Processing**:
   - o Add a loop to apply watermarks to all images in a folder, allowing for batch watermarking.

- o **Example**: Process all images in a directory.

```python
Copy code
import os

def batch_watermark(input_folder, watermark_path, output_folder):
    for filename in os.listdir(input_folder):
        if filename.endswith(".jpg") or filename.endswith(".png"):
            input_path = os.path.join(input_folder, filename)
            output_path = os.path.join(output_folder, f"watermarked_{filename}")
            apply_watermark(input_path, watermark_path, output_path)

batch_watermark("input_images", "watermark.png", "output_images")
```

2. **Custom Watermark Text**:
   - o Generate a text-based watermark using Pillow's ImageDraw and ImageFont classes. This could be useful for adding dynamic text watermarks like dates or usernames.

3. **Adding Filters or Enhancements**:
   - ○ Apply filters (e.g., grayscale) or adjust image brightness and contrast before watermarking for added customization.

4. **Transparency Detection**:
   - ○ Detect the presence of a transparent background in the watermark image, adjusting placement or color for better visibility on different backgrounds.

In this chapter, you explored the basics of image processing with Pillow, covering tasks like resizing, cropping, and applying filters to images. We built an automated watermarking tool that can be used to protect intellectual property or brand content. Pillow's flexibility makes it an excellent choice for automating repetitive image editing tasks.

In the next chapter, we'll discuss web automation and data collection with APIs, which enables you to integrate your Python scripts with other online services and automate workflows across platforms.

CHAPTER 15: DATA VISUALIZATION AND REPORTING AUTOMATION

Data visualization is crucial for understanding and communicating insights effectively. Automating the generation of reports with charts can save time and improve consistency, especially in data-driven fields. In this chapter, you'll learn to create visualizations with **Matplotlib**, automate report generation with data visuals, and build an example project that produces an automated monthly data report.

Creating Charts and Graphs with Matplotlib

Matplotlib is a powerful library for creating static, animated, and interactive visualizations in Python. With it, you can create a wide range of charts, including line plots, bar charts, pie charts, and histograms.

1. **Installing Matplotlib**:
    - If you haven't already, install Matplotlib using pip:

    bash
    Copy code
    pip install matplotlib

2. **Basic Line Plot**:

- ○ Line plots are ideal for displaying trends over time, such as monthly sales or website traffic.
- ○ **Example**: Plotting monthly sales data.

python

Copy code

```
import matplotlib.pyplot as plt

months = ["January", "February", "March", "April", "May"]
sales = [1000, 1500, 1200, 1700, 1600]

plt.plot(months, sales, marker="o")
plt.title("Monthly Sales Data")
plt.xlabel("Months")
plt.ylabel("Sales ($)")
plt.show()
```

3. **Bar Chart**:
   - ○ Bar charts are useful for comparing categories, like product sales or survey responses.
   - ○ **Example**: Plotting sales by product.

python

Copy code

```
products = ["Product A", "Product B", "Product C"]
```

```
sales = [300, 500, 700]
```

```
plt.bar(products, sales, color="skyblue")
plt.title("Sales by Product")
plt.xlabel("Products")
plt.ylabel("Sales ($)")
plt.show()
```

4. **Pie Chart**:
   - o Pie charts display proportions of a whole, making them suitable for showing market share, budget allocation, etc.
   - o **Example**: Displaying market share.

   ```python
   Copy code
   labels = ["Company A", "Company B", "Company C"]
   market_share = [50, 30, 20]

   plt.pie(market_share, labels=labels, autopct="%1.1f%%", startangle=140)
   plt.title("Market Share")
   plt.show()
   ```

5. **Histogram**:

- o Histograms show the distribution of data, ideal for visualizing ranges like age groups or income levels.
- o **Example**: Plotting income distribution.

```python
Copy code
import numpy as np

income_data = np.random.normal(50000, 10000, 1000)
plt.hist(income_data, bins=30, color="purple", edgecolor="black")
plt.title("Income Distribution")
plt.xlabel("Income")
plt.ylabel("Frequency")
plt.show()
```

Automating Report Generation with Visuals

Automated report generation combines data processing, visualization, and document creation. By automating this process, you can produce consistent, up-to-date reports with minimal effort.

1. **Generating and Saving Charts Programmatically**:
   - o Instead of displaying charts with plt.show(), you can save them as image files to include in reports.
   - o **Example**: Saving a chart as an image.

```
python
Copy code
plt.plot(months, sales, marker="o")
plt.title("Monthly Sales Data")
plt.xlabel("Months")
plt.ylabel("Sales ($)")
plt.savefig("monthly_sales_chart.png")
plt.close()  # Close the plot to avoid reusing it
```

2. **Creating Reports with Data Visuals**:
   - ○ Using python-docx, you can create a Word document and insert the saved charts into the report.
   - ○ **Example**: Adding a chart image to a Word document.

```
python
Copy code
from docx import Document
from docx.shared import Inches

# Create a new document
doc = Document()
doc.add_heading("Monthly Sales Report", level=1)

# Add a paragraph and insert the chart image
```

```
doc.add_paragraph("The following chart shows the
monthly sales trend:")
doc.add_picture("monthly_sales_chart.png",
width=Inches(5))

# Save the document
doc.save("monthly_sales_report.docx")
```

Example Project: Automated Monthly Data Report with Charts

Let's create a script that automates the generation of a monthly report, complete with data visualizations. The report will include sales data, a summary table, and charts to illustrate trends and comparisons.

1. **Project Overview**:
   - The script will pull sales data for each month, generate visualizations, and create a Word document report.
   - The report will include a title, introductory paragraph, bar and line charts, and a summary table.
2. **Preparing Sample Data**:
   - **Example data**: Monthly sales data for three products.

   python

```
Copy code
import pandas as pd

# Sample data
data = {
    "Month":   ["January",  "February",   "March",
"April", "May"],
    "Product A": [1000, 1100, 1200, 1300, 1400],
    "Product B": [900, 950, 970, 980, 1000],
    "Product C": [850, 800, 750, 780, 800]
}
sales_data = pd.DataFrame(data)
```

3. **Writing the Report Generation Script**:

```python
Copy code
import matplotlib.pyplot as plt
from docx import Document
from docx.shared import Inches

def generate_sales_charts(data):
    # Line chart for monthly sales trends
    plt.figure()
    for product in ["Product A", "Product B", "Product C"]:
```

```
    plt.plot(data["Month"],    data[product],    marker="o",
label=product)
  plt.title("Monthly Sales Trends")
  plt.xlabel("Month")
  plt.ylabel("Sales ($)")
  plt.legend()
  plt.savefig("sales_trends_chart.png")
  plt.close()


  # Bar chart for total sales by product
  total_sales = data[["Product A", "Product B", "Product
C"]].sum()
  plt.figure()
  plt.bar(total_sales.index,                total_sales.values,
color=["skyblue", "salmon", "lightgreen"])
  plt.title("Total Sales by Product")
  plt.xlabel("Products")
  plt.ylabel("Total Sales ($)")
  plt.savefig("total_sales_chart.png")
  plt.close()


def create_report(data):
  # Create a new Word document
  doc = Document()
  doc.add_heading("Monthly Sales Report", level=1)
```

```python
doc.add_paragraph("This report provides an overview of
monthly sales performance, including trends and total sales
by product.")

# Add charts to the report
doc.add_paragraph("1. Monthly Sales Trends")
doc.add_picture("sales_trends_chart.png",
width=Inches(5))

doc.add_paragraph("2. Total Sales by Product")
doc.add_picture("total_sales_chart.png",
width=Inches(5))

# Add a data summary table
doc.add_heading("Sales Data Summary", level=2)
table = doc.add_table(rows=1, cols=len(data.columns))
hdr_cells = table.rows[0].cells
for i, column_name in enumerate(data.columns):
    hdr_cells[i].text = column_name

for index, row in data.iterrows():
    row_cells = table.add_row().cells
    for i, value in enumerate(row):
        row_cells[i].text = str(value)
```

```
# Save the document
filename = "monthly_sales_report.docx"
doc.save(filename)
print(f"Report saved as {filename}")


# Generate charts and create the report
generate_sales_charts(sales_data)
create_report(sales_data)
```

4. **Explanation of the Script**:
   - **generate_sales_charts**: Creates two charts (a line chart for trends and a bar chart for total sales), saves them as images, and closes each figure.
   - **create_report**: Creates a Word document, adds the saved charts, and generates a summary table from the data.
   - **Adding Tables and Images**: The table displays sales for each month by product, while the images illustrate trends and totals visually.

5. **Running the Script**:
   - Save the code as monthly_report_generator.py and run it:

   bash
   Copy code
   python monthly_report_generator.py

o The script will create monthly_sales_report.docx, which contains the sales data summary, line chart, and bar chart.

6. **Sample Output**:

   o The generated Word document will contain:

      ▪ A title and introductory paragraph.

      ▪ A line chart showing monthly sales trends.

      ▪ A bar chart displaying total sales by product.

      ▪ A summary table of monthly sales data.

Further Enhancements

1. **Integrate Real-Time Data**:

   o Pull data from a database, API, or CSV file for automated reports with real-time updates.

2. **Emailing the Report**:

   o After generating the report, automate sending it via email using smtplib.

3. **Customizable Reporting Options**:

   o Allow users to choose reporting time frames (weekly, monthly, quarterly) and customize the charts.

4. **Add Data Insights**:

   o Use Python to calculate key performance indicators (KPIs) and display insights in the report (e.g., average sales growth, best-performing product).

In this chapter, you learned how to create data visualizations with Matplotlib and integrate them into automated reports using python-docx. The example project demonstrated how to build a monthly report with line and bar charts, along with a data summary table. Automating report generation is a valuable skill in data analytics, enabling you to produce timely, professional reports with minimal manual effort.

In the next chapter, we'll discuss data collection from APIs, allowing you to access and incorporate real-time data into your Python automation projects.

CHAPTER 16: AUTOMATING DESKTOP APPLICATIONS WITH PYAUTOGUI

Automating desktop applications can save time on repetitive tasks, such as data entry, software navigation, and file management. **PyAutoGUI** is a Python library that enables you to control your mouse and keyboard, allowing for automation of any graphical user interface (GUI) task. In this chapter, we'll explore the basics of PyAutoGUI, learn to automate mouse movements and keyboard actions, and build a practical example for automating repetitive GUI tasks.

Introduction to GUI Automation with PyAutoGUI

1. **What is PyAutoGUI?**
   - PyAutoGUI is a cross-platform library for GUI automation in Python. It can simulate mouse movements, clicks, and keyboard presses, making it possible to automate any application you can navigate manually.
   - **Use Cases**:
     - Automating form entries in desktop applications.

- Navigating software interfaces, like clicking menus or selecting options.
- Interacting with non-web applications that don't have APIs for automation.

2. **Installing PyAutoGUI**:
   o Install PyAutoGUI using pip:

   bash

   Copy code

   pip install pyautogui

3. **Basic Safety and Precautions**:
   o **Failsafe**: PyAutoGUI has a failsafe feature where moving the mouse to the top-left corner of the screen will terminate the script.
   o **Delays**: Add delays between commands to prevent the automation from running too fast, allowing you to intervene if needed.

python

Copy code

import pyautogui

pyautogui.FAILSAFE = True # Enable failsafe
pyautogui.PAUSE = 0.5 # Pause for 0.5 seconds after each PyAutoGUI call

Automating Mouse Movements and Keyboard Actions

PyAutoGUI offers a variety of methods for controlling the mouse and keyboard, including moving the mouse, clicking, typing, and taking screenshots.

1. **Mouse Movements and Clicking**:
   - **Moving the Mouse**: Use moveTo(x, y) to move the mouse to a specific screen coordinate, or move(x, y) to move relative to the current position.
   - **Clicking**: Use click() to perform a click, with options for button (left, right, middle) and click count (e.g., double-click).

python
Copy code
```
# Move the mouse to position (100, 200) and left-click
pyautogui.moveTo(100, 200)
pyautogui.click()

# Right-click at the current position
pyautogui.rightClick()

# Double-click at the current position
pyautogui.doubleClick()
```

2. **Dragging and Scrolling**:

- o **Dragging**: Use dragTo() or drag() to drag the mouse to a location. This is useful for selecting text or moving files.
- o **Scrolling**: Use scroll() to scroll up or down by a specified amount.

python

Copy code

```
# Drag from the current position to (300, 400)
pyautogui.dragTo(300, 400, duration=0.5)


# Scroll up 500 units
pyautogui.scroll(500)
```

3. **Typing and Pressing Keys**:
   - o **Typing Text**: Use typewrite() to type a string as if typing on the keyboard. You can also specify a delay between each keystroke.
   - o **Pressing Individual Keys**: Use press() for single keystrokes or hotkey() for combinations like Ctrl+C.

python

Copy code

```
# Type text with a delay of 0.1 seconds between each
character
pyautogui.typewrite("Hello, world!", interval=0.1)
```

```
# Press Enter
pyautogui.press("enter")


# Press a combination of keys (e.g., Ctrl+C to copy)
pyautogui.hotkey("ctrl", "c")
```

4. **Taking Screenshots**:
   - Screenshots can help verify if the automation is in the right place or capture data from the screen.
   - **Example**: Taking a screenshot and saving it as a file.

python
Copy code
```
screenshot = pyautogui.screenshot()
screenshot.save("screenshot.png")
```

5. **Finding Screen Elements with Image Recognition**:
   - Use locateOnScreen() to find the coordinates of an image on the screen, like a button or icon. This is useful for locating elements to interact with.
   - **Example**: Clicking on an icon if it's found on the screen.

   python
   Copy code

```
button_location                                    =
pyautogui.locateOnScreen("button_image.png")
if button_location:
    button_center                                  =
pyautogui.center(button_location)
        pyautogui.click(button_center)
else:
        print("Button not found on screen.")
```

Real-World Application: Automating Repetitive GUI Tasks

Let's build a script to automate filling out a form on a desktop application or website. This example will demonstrate using mouse clicks, typing, and navigation to perform tasks that would otherwise require manual interaction.

1. **Project Overview**:
   - The task involves filling out a form with fields like Name, Email, and Message.
   - The script will locate each field, enter the necessary information, and submit the form.
2. **Preparing for Automation**:
   - Capture screenshots of each input field or button (if image recognition is needed).
   - Plan the sequence of actions to be performed, including pauses where necessary.

3. **Writing the Form Automation Script**:

```python
python
Copy code
import pyautogui
import time

# Coordinates of form fields and button (adjust these based
on your screen resolution)
name_field = (200, 300)
email_field = (200, 350)
message_field = (200, 400)
submit_button = (200, 450)

# Data to enter
name = "John Doe"
email = "john.doe@example.com"
message = "This is an automated message sent by a Python
script."

# Function to fill out the form
def fill_form():
    # Move to the name field, click, and type the name
    pyautogui.click(name_field)
    pyautogui.typewrite(name, interval=0.1)
```

```
    # Move to the email field, click, and type the email
    pyautogui.click(email_field)
    pyautogui.typewrite(email, interval=0.1)

    # Move to the message field, click, and type the message
    pyautogui.click(message_field)
    pyautogui.typewrite(message, interval=0.1)

    # Move to the submit button and click it
    pyautogui.click(submit_button)
    print("Form submitted successfully!")

# Run the form-filling automation
fill_form()
```

4. **Explanation of the Script**:
   - **Coordinates**: Coordinates for each field are defined based on the screen resolution. You may need to adjust these values to match your setup.
   - **Typing Data**: The typewrite() function types each piece of information into the form fields.
   - **Submitting the Form**: The script clicks the submit button after entering all data.

5. **Running the Script**:
   - Save the code as form_automation.py and run it:

bash

Copy code

python form_automation.py

- o The script will automatically fill out the form and submit it. Ensure the form window is open and visible on your screen before running the script.

6. **Sample Output**:

css

Copy code

Form submitted successfully!

Further Enhancements

1. **Dynamic Element Detection**:
   - o Instead of hardcoding coordinates, use image recognition (locateOnScreen()) to dynamically locate elements. This makes the script adaptable to screen changes.

2. **Error Handling and Verification**:
   - o Add checks to verify if fields are correctly filled and the form was submitted. Capture screenshots or confirm by checking for specific screen elements after submission.

3. **Batch Processing**:

- o Extend the script to fill multiple forms or submit different sets of data from a CSV or database.

4. **Automating Desktop Software**:
   - o Use PyAutoGUI to automate repetitive software tasks, such as generating reports, converting files, or navigating through menus.

5. **Scheduling and Timing**:
   - o Combine with scheduling libraries to automate tasks at specific times, like batch data entries or software updates.

In this chapter, you explored GUI automation with PyAutoGUI, covering basics like mouse movements, keyboard actions, and image recognition. You learned to automate a form submission task, illustrating the potential of PyAutoGUI for desktop automation. This skill is valuable for handling repetitive tasks across various applications, enhancing productivity and minimizing manual work.

In the next chapter, we'll cover database automation, where you'll learn to connect to databases, query data, and automate data operations for seamless data management workflows.

CHAPTER 17: HANDLING ERRORS AND LOGGING

Effective error handling and logging are essential in automation scripts, as they ensure smooth operation, help identify issues, and provide transparency in long-running or unattended processes. In this chapter, you'll learn how to manage exceptions, debug scripts, and set up logging for automated processes. We'll also create a practical example of adding logging to a file management automation script.

Managing Exceptions and Debugging Scripts

1. **Understanding Exceptions in Python**:
   - Exceptions are errors that occur during the execution of a program. Handling them prevents your script from crashing and allows you to respond to issues more gracefully.
   - **Common Exceptions**:
     - **FileNotFoundError**: Raised when trying to access a file that doesn't exist.
     - **ValueError**: Raised when a function receives an argument of the right type but inappropriate value.
     - **KeyError**: Raised when trying to access a dictionary key that doesn't exist.

2. **Using Try-Except Blocks**:

    o   A **try-except** block allows you to attempt an operation and catch specific exceptions if they occur, letting your script continue executing or perform alternative actions.

    o   **Example**: Handling file errors.

    python
    Copy code
    ```
    try:
        with open("nonexistent_file.txt", "r") as file:
            content = file.read()
    except FileNotFoundError:
        print("The file was not found.")
    ```

3. **Catching Multiple Exceptions**:

    o   You can catch multiple types of exceptions by specifying them in parentheses, or using a general Exception to catch all errors (use sparingly for better debugging).

    o   **Example**: Handling multiple exception types.

    python
    Copy code
    ```
    try:
        result = int("abc")
    ```

```
except (ValueError, TypeError) as e:
    print(f"An error occurred: {e}")
```

4. **Using the Finally Block**:
   - o The **finally** block runs regardless of whether an exception was raised. It's ideal for cleanup tasks, like closing a file or database connection.
   - o **Example**: Using finally for resource cleanup.

   python
   Copy code
   ```
   try:
       file = open("example.txt", "r")
       content = file.read()
   except Exception as e:
       print(f"An error occurred: {e}")
   finally:
       file.close()
   ```

5. **Raising Custom Exceptions**:
   - o If a specific condition is met, you can raise your own exceptions using raise, which helps create clear and customized error messages.
   - o **Example**: Raising a custom exception.

   python
   Copy code

```
def check_age(age):
    if age < 0:
        raise ValueError("Age cannot be negative.")
    return age


try:
    check_age(-5)
except ValueError as e:
    print(e)
```

Setting Up Logging for Automated Processes

The **logging** module in Python provides a way to record messages from your program, ranging from debugging information to critical errors. Logging helps monitor the performance and stability of your automation scripts.

1. **Basic Logging Configuration**:
   - The logging.basicConfig() function allows you to set up a basic configuration, including the logging level, format, and file for log messages.
   - **Example**: Setting up basic logging to log messages to a file.

   python
   Copy code
   ```
   import logging
   ```

```
logging.basicConfig(
    filename="app.log",
    level=logging.DEBUG,
    format="%(asctime)s   -   %(levelname)s   -
%(message)s"
)
```

2. **Logging Levels**:
   - Python's logging module has several levels, each representing the severity of the event:
     - **DEBUG**: Detailed information, useful for diagnosing issues.
     - **INFO**: Confirmation that things are working as expected.
     - **WARNING**: An indication of potential issues that don't interrupt the program.
     - **ERROR**: A more serious issue that affects functionality.
     - **CRITICAL**: A severe error that likely stops the program.
   - **Example**: Logging messages at different levels.

   python
   Copy code
   ```
   logging.debug("This is a debug message.")
   ```

```
logging.info("This is an info message.")
logging.warning("This is a warning message.")
logging.error("This is an error message.")
logging.critical("This is a critical message.")
```

3. **Using Loggers, Handlers, and Formatters**:
   - **Logger**: The main object for logging messages.
   - **Handler**: Specifies where logs go, such as a file or console.
   - **Formatter**: Defines the log message format.
   - **Example**: Setting up custom logging with a file handler and custom format.

   python
   Copy code

```
logger = logging.getLogger("file_management")
handler =
logging.FileHandler("file_management.log")
formatter = logging.Formatter("%(asctime)s -
%(name)s - %(levelname)s - %(message)s")
handler.setFormatter(formatter)
logger.addHandler(handler)
logger.setLevel(logging.INFO)

# Log a message
logger.info("File management process started.")
```

Practical Example: Logging for a File Management Automation Script

Let's create a file management script that organizes files in a folder based on their file type (e.g., images, documents, videos). We'll add logging to record each step, error, and outcome.

1. **Project Overview**:
   - The script will scan a specified directory, create folders based on file types, and move files to their respective folders.
   - Logs will record each file move and capture any errors encountered.
2. **File Organization Script with Logging**:

```python
Copy code
import os
import shutil
import logging

# Setup logging
logging.basicConfig(
    filename="file_organizer.log",
    level=logging.INFO,
    format="%(asctime)s - %(levelname)s - %(message)s"
)
```

```python
# Directory to organize
source_directory = "source_folder"

# Define categories for different file types
file_types = {
    "Images": [".jpg", ".jpeg", ".png", ".gif"],
    "Documents": [".pdf", ".docx", ".txt", ".xlsx"],
    "Videos": [".mp4", ".mov", ".avi"],
    "Archives": [".zip", ".tar", ".gz"]
}

# Create folders for each category
def create_folders():
    for folder in file_types.keys():
        folder_path = os.path.join(source_directory, folder)
        if not os.path.exists(folder_path):
            os.makedirs(folder_path)
            logging.info(f"Created folder: {folder_path}")

# Function to organize files
def organize_files():
    try:
        for filename in os.listdir(source_directory):
            file_path = os.path.join(source_directory, filename)
```

```python
        # Skip directories
        if os.path.isdir(file_path):
            continue

        # Identify file type and move to the appropriate
folder
        moved = False
        for folder, extensions in file_types.items():
            if any(filename.lower().endswith(ext) for ext in
extensions):
                target_path    =    os.path.join(source_directory,
folder, filename)
                shutil.move(file_path, target_path)
                logging.info(f"Moved    file:    {filename}    to
{folder}")
                moved = True
                break

        # Log files that don't match any category
        if not moved:
            logging.warning(f"Uncategorized                file:
{filename}")

    except Exception as e:
```

```
        logging.error(f"Error organizing files: {e}")


# Run the folder creation and organization
if __name__ == "__main__":
    logging.info("Starting file organization process.")
    create_folders()
    organize_files()
    logging.info("File organization process completed.")
```

3. **Explanation of the Script**:

   o **Folder Creation**: The create_folders() function creates folders for each file category and logs each new folder.

   o **File Organization**: The organize_files() function checks each file's extension, moves it to the correct folder, and logs the action. Files that don't match any category trigger a warning message.

   o **Error Handling**: The script uses a try-except block in organize_files() to log any errors during file organization.

4. **Running the Script**:

   o Save the code as file_organizer.py and create a folder named source_folder with sample files. Run the script:

   bash

Copy code

python file_organizer.py

5. **Log File Output**:

   o The generated file_organizer.log file might look like this:

   yaml

   Copy code

   2023-11-01 12:00:00 - INFO - Starting file organization process.

   2023-11-01 12:00:00 - INFO - Created folder: source_folder/Images

   2023-11-01 12:00:01 - INFO - Moved file: picture.jpg to Images

   2023-11-01 12:00:01 - WARNING - Uncategorized file: notes.tmp

   2023-11-01 12:00:02 - INFO - File organization process completed.

Further Enhancements

1. **Logging Rotation**:

   o Use logging.handlers.RotatingFileHandler to automatically rotate log files when they reach a specific size, preventing logs from growing too large.

2. **Detailed Error Messages**:
   - o Include exception details (e.g., str(e)) for more informative error logs.

3. **Integrate with Notifications**:
   - o Add email notifications or SMS alerts when errors occur in critical automation tasks, using services like SMTP or Twilio.

4. **Summary Logs**:
   - o Log summary information, like the total number of files processed, the number of errors, or files moved, to help with performance tracking.

In this chapter, you learned how to manage errors, debug scripts, and set up logging in Python automation projects. With effective logging, you can monitor the progress and performance of your scripts, ensuring smoother operation and easier troubleshooting. The practical example of a file management automation script demonstrated how logging adds value by tracking each action and error encountered, making automation workflows more reliable.

In the next chapter, we'll explore data automation with databases, covering how to connect, query, and manipulate data in SQL databases to streamline data management tasks.

CHAPTER 18: INTEGRATING DATABASES FOR AUTOMATION

Databases provide a reliable way to store, manage, and retrieve structured data, making them essential for many automation tasks. By integrating databases into your Python scripts, you can automate data storage, retrieval, and manipulation, enabling more sophisticated workflows. In this chapter, we'll cover basic database operations using **SQLite** and **MySQL**, discuss storing and retrieving data, and create an example of automating customer data storage and retrieval.

Basic Database Operations with SQLite and MySQL

1. **Choosing Between SQLite and MySQL**:
   - **SQLite**: Lightweight, file-based, and great for small projects or local applications. No setup is required beyond Python's sqlite3 library.
   - **MySQL**: A more robust, server-based database suitable for larger applications, remote access, and concurrent users. Requires MySQL server setup.

2. **Setting Up SQLite**:
   - SQLite comes with Python, so no additional installation is required. You can start using it with the sqlite3 library.

- o **Example**: Connecting to an SQLite database and creating a table.

```python
Copy code
import sqlite3

# Connect to a SQLite database (or create it if it doesn't exist)
conn = sqlite3.connect("customer_data.db")
cursor = conn.cursor()

# Create a table
cursor.execute("""
CREATE TABLE IF NOT EXISTS customers (
    id INTEGER PRIMARY KEY AUTOINCREMENT,
    name TEXT NOT NULL,
    email TEXT NOT NULL UNIQUE,
    join_date TEXT NOT NULL
)
""")
conn.commit()
```

3. **Setting Up MySQL**:

- To use MySQL, install the mysql-connector-python package:

bash
Copy code

```
pip install mysql-connector-python
```

- **Example**: Connecting to a MySQL database and creating a table.

python
Copy code

```
import mysql.connector

# Connect to a MySQL database
conn = mysql.connector.connect(
    host="localhost",
    user="your_username",
    password="your_password",
    database="your_database"
)
cursor = conn.cursor()

# Create a table
cursor.execute("""
CREATE TABLE IF NOT EXISTS customers (
```

```
        id INT AUTO_INCREMENT PRIMARY KEY,
        name VARCHAR(100),
        email VARCHAR(100) UNIQUE,
        join_date DATE
    )
    """)
    conn.commit()
```

Storing and Retrieving Data for Automated Tasks

Databases are ideal for storing data in a structured way, making it easy to retrieve and update information for automated workflows.

1. **Inserting Data into a Database**:
   - Use INSERT INTO statements to add records. Placeholders (e.g., ? in SQLite, %s in MySQL) help protect against SQL injection attacks.
   - **Example**: Inserting a customer's data.

   python
   Copy code
   ```python
   # Insert a new customer record
   customer_data = ("Alice Johnson", "alice@example.com", "2023-11-01")
   cursor.execute("INSERT INTO customers (name, email, join_date) VALUES (?, ?, ?)", customer_data)
   ```

```python
conn.commit()
```

2. **Retrieving Data from a Database**:
   - ○ Use SELECT statements to query data. You can filter data with WHERE clauses and order results with ORDER BY.
   - ○ **Example**: Retrieving all customer records.

   ```python
   python
   Copy code
   cursor.execute("SELECT * FROM customers")
   customers = cursor.fetchall()
   for customer in customers:
       print(customer)
   ```

3. **Updating and Deleting Records**:
   - ○ **Updating**: Use UPDATE to modify existing records.
   - ○ **Deleting**: Use DELETE FROM to remove records based on conditions.
   - ○ **Example**: Updating and deleting customer data.

   ```python
   python
   Copy code
   # Update a customer's email
   ```

```
cursor.execute("UPDATE customers SET email = ?
WHERE name = ?", ("new_email@example.com",
"Alice Johnson"))
conn.commit()

# Delete a customer record
cursor.execute("DELETE     FROM     customers
WHERE name = ?", ("Alice Johnson",))
conn.commit()
```

4. **Using Transactions for Data Integrity**:
   - o Transactions ensure that a group of database operations are treated as a single unit, which is important for data consistency.
   - o Start with BEGIN TRANSACTION, execute statements, and commit with conn.commit(). If an error occurs, use conn.rollback() to revert changes.

Example: Automating Customer Data Storage and Retrieval

In this example, we'll build a Python script that automates the process of storing new customer data and retrieving a list of all customers. The script will use SQLite, but the same structure applies to MySQL with minor adjustments.

1. **Project Overview**:

- o The script will prompt the user to enter customer data and store it in the database.
- o It will also provide an option to retrieve and display all customer records.

2. **Writing the Automation Script**:

```python
Copy code
import sqlite3
from datetime import datetime

# Connect to the database
conn = sqlite3.connect("customer_data.db")
cursor = conn.cursor()

# Create the customers table if it doesn't exist
cursor.execute("""
CREATE TABLE IF NOT EXISTS customers (
    id INTEGER PRIMARY KEY AUTOINCREMENT,
    name TEXT NOT NULL,
    email TEXT NOT NULL UNIQUE,
    join_date TEXT NOT NULL
)
""")
conn.commit()
```

```python
# Function to add a new customer
def add_customer(name, email):
    join_date = datetime.now().strftime("%Y-%m-%d")
    try:
        cursor.execute("INSERT INTO customers (name, email, join_date) VALUES (?, ?, ?)", (name, email, join_date))
        conn.commit()
        print(f"Customer {name} added successfully.")
    except sqlite3.IntegrityError:
        print("Error: A customer with that email already exists.")


# Function to retrieve all customers
def get_customers():
    cursor.execute("SELECT * FROM customers")
    customers = cursor.fetchall()
    print("Customer List:")
    for customer in customers:
        print(customer)


# Main menu for the automation script
def main():
    while True:
        print("\nCustomer Data Automation")
```

```python
    print("1. Add New Customer")
    print("2. View All Customers")
    print("3. Exit")

    choice = input("Enter your choice: ")
    if choice == "1":
        name = input("Enter customer's name: ")
        email = input("Enter customer's email: ")
        add_customer(name, email)
    elif choice == "2":
        get_customers()
    elif choice == "3":
        break
    else:
        print("Invalid choice. Please try again.")

# Run the main menu
if __name__ == "__main__":
    main()
    conn.close()
```

3. **Explanation of the Script**:

    o **add_customer**: Inserts a new customer into the database with a timestamp. It catches duplicate email entries using sqlite3.IntegrityError.

- o **get_customers**: Queries all records from the customers table and displays each customer's details.
- o **Main Menu**: Provides a simple interface to add customers, view all customers, or exit the script.

4. **Running the Script**:

- o Save the code as customer_management.py and run it:

bash

Copy code

python customer_management.py

5. **Sample Output**:

- o When you choose to add a new customer or view all customers, the script will display the data from the database:

python

Copy code

Customer Data Automation

1. Add New Customer

2. View All Customers

3. Exit

Enter your choice: 1

Enter customer's name: Alice Johnson

Enter customer's email: alice.johnson@example.com

Customer Alice Johnson added successfully.

Enter your choice: 2

Customer List:

(1, 'Alice Johnson', 'alice.johnson@example.com', '2023-11-01')

Further Enhancements

1. **Switching to MySQL**:
   - Adapt the script for MySQL by changing the connection setup and minor adjustments to SQL syntax.

2. **Batch Data Import**:
   - Allow the script to read customer data from a CSV file and batch-insert it into the database.

3. **Data Validation**:
   - Add input validation to check for valid email addresses and prevent duplicate records based on email.

4. **Automated Reporting**:

      o Integrate with data visualization libraries (e.g., Matplotlib) to create automated reports on customer data (e.g., new customers per month).

5. **Advanced Queries**:

      o Implement more complex queries, such as filtering customers based on join date or querying based on specific criteria (e.g., last month's new customers).

In this chapter, you learned how to integrate databases into your automation scripts, covering essential operations with SQLite and MySQL. Databases provide a powerful solution for storing and retrieving data in an organized manner, allowing for efficient and reliable data automation. The example project demonstrated automating customer data storage and retrieval, a common requirement in CRM systems and data management tasks.

In the next chapter, we'll cover API integration for data automation, which allows you to connect your Python scripts to web services, retrieve real-time data, and automate web-based workflows.

CHAPTER 19: BUILDING A COMPLETE AUTOMATION PROJECT

In this chapter, we'll bring together the techniques covered in previous chapters to plan and execute a complete automation project. We'll discuss best practices for planning and structuring larger projects, outline how to integrate multiple automation techniques, and provide a step-by-step example of creating an **Automated Task Manager**. This project will incorporate reminders, alerts, and task tracking.

Planning and Structuring a Larger Automation Project

Building a larger automation project requires careful planning, modularity, and testing to ensure that all components work together seamlessly.

1. **Define the Project Requirements**:

- o Determine what the project needs to accomplish, including core functions and additional features.
- o For our Automated Task Manager, core functions might include:
  - Creating, updating, and deleting tasks.
  - Setting due dates and reminders.
  - Sending alerts (e.g., email or SMS) for upcoming deadlines.
  - Tracking task completion and providing summaries.

2. **Break the Project into Modules**:
   - o Modularize the project to ensure maintainability and flexibility.
   - o Suggested modules for an Automated Task Manager:
     - **Database Module**: Stores tasks and tracks their status.
     - **Reminder Module**: Schedules reminders and sends alerts.
     - **User Interface Module**: Provides an interface for users to add, update, and view tasks (could be console-based or GUI).
     - **Scheduler Module**: Runs the automation at specified intervals (e.g., daily or hourly).

3. **Choose the Right Tools and Libraries**:

- o Select libraries and tools that fit the project's needs:
    - **Database**: SQLite or MySQL for storing tasks.
    - **Scheduling**: schedule or APScheduler for task scheduling.
    - **Notifications**: smtplib for emails, Twilio for SMS, and logging for tracking activity.

4. **Design Data Models and Structures**:
    - o Design tables or data structures to store information efficiently. For example:
        - Task table with columns for ID, name, description, due date, priority, status, and reminder time.
        - A reminders table to manage pending reminders if needed.

5. **Implement Testing and Error Handling**:
    - o Add error handling for database connections, scheduling issues, and message delivery.
    - o Design unit tests for each module to ensure each component functions as expected.

Combining Multiple Automation Techniques in One Project

This project will integrate several automation techniques:

1. **Database Operations**:

- o Use SQLite to store task details, including task name, description, due date, and status.
- o Enable adding, updating, deleting, and querying tasks.

2. **Scheduling Reminders**:
   - o Use schedule to set up daily reminders for tasks due on the current or following day.

3. **Sending Alerts**:
   - o Send email or SMS alerts for tasks nearing their due dates using smtplib (for email) and Twilio (for SMS).

4. **Logging**:
   - o Implement logging to record task activity, such as tasks created, reminders sent, and tasks completed.

Example Project: Automated Task Manager

Let's create an automated task manager that:

- Stores tasks in a database.
- Schedules reminders for upcoming tasks.
- Sends alerts as email or SMS notifications for tasks approaching their due dates.
- Tracks task completion and provides summary reports.

Step 1: Set Up the Database

python

Copy code

```
import sqlite3

# Connect to the database and create tasks table
conn = sqlite3.connect("tasks.db")
cursor = conn.cursor()

cursor.execute("""
CREATE TABLE IF NOT EXISTS tasks (
    id INTEGER PRIMARY KEY AUTOINCREMENT,
    name TEXT NOT NULL,
    description TEXT,
    due_date TEXT,
    priority INTEGER,
    status TEXT DEFAULT 'Pending',
    reminder_time TEXT
)
""")
conn.commit()
```

Step 2: Add Functions for Managing Tasks

python

Copy code

```
from datetime import datetime

# Function to add a new task
```

```python
def add_task(name, description, due_date, priority, reminder_time):
    cursor.execute("""
    INSERT INTO tasks (name, description, due_date, priority, reminder_time)
    VALUES (?, ?, ?, ?, ?)
    """, (name, description, due_date, priority, reminder_time))
    conn.commit()
    print(f"Task '{name}' added successfully.")


# Function to update a task's status
def mark_task_complete(task_id):
    cursor.execute("UPDATE tasks SET status = 'Complete' WHERE id = ?", (task_id,))
    conn.commit()
    print(f"Task with ID {task_id} marked as complete.")


# Function to retrieve all pending tasks
def get_pending_tasks():
    cursor.execute("SELECT * FROM tasks WHERE status = 'Pending'")
    return cursor.fetchall()
```

Step 3: Schedule Reminders and Alerts

python

Copy code

```python
import schedule
import time
import logging
from datetime import datetime, timedelta


# Configure logging
logging.basicConfig(filename="task_manager.log",
level=logging.INFO, format="%(asctime)s - %(message)s")


# Function to send reminders (dummy function for demonstration)
def send_reminder(task):
    print(f"Reminder: Task '{task[1]}' is due on {task[3]}")
    logging.info(f"Sent reminder for task '{task[1]}' due on
{task[3]}")


# Function to check for tasks due soon and send reminders
def check_due_tasks():
    pending_tasks = get_pending_tasks()
    for task in pending_tasks:
        due_date = datetime.strptime(task[3], "%Y-%m-%d")
        reminder_date = due_date - timedelta(days=1)  # Set reminder
one day before due date
        if datetime.now().date() == reminder_date.date():
            send_reminder(task)
```

```
# Schedule the reminder checker to run every day at a set time
schedule.every().day.at("08:00").do(check_due_tasks)


# Run the scheduler
def run_scheduler():
    while True:
        schedule.run_pending()
        time.sleep(60)  # Check every minute
```

Step 4: Sending Email Alerts

python
Copy code

```
import smtplib
from email.mime.text import MIMEText
from email.mime.multipart import MIMEMultipart


# Function to send an email alert for an upcoming task
def send_email_alert(task, recipient_email):
    sender_email = "your_email@example.com"
    password = "your_password"

    subject = f"Reminder: Task '{task[1]}' Due Soon"
    body = f"Hello,\n\nThis is a reminder that the task '{task[1]}' is due on {task[3]}.\n\nTask Description: {task[2]}"

    message = MIMEMultipart()
```

```python
message["From"] = sender_email
message["To"] = recipient_email
message["Subject"] = subject
message.attach(MIMEText(body, "plain"))


try:
    with smtplib.SMTP("smtp.gmail.com", 587) as server:
        server.starttls()
        server.login(sender_email, password)
        server.sendmail(sender_email,          recipient_email,
message.as_string())
        logging.info(f"Email    sent    for    task    '{task[1]}'    to
{recipient_email}")
    except Exception as e:
        logging.error(f"Failed to send email for task '{task[1]}': {e}")
```

Step 5: Running the Automated Task Manager

python

Copy code

```python
if __name__ == "__main__":
    # Sample task addition (could be from user input or CSV)
    add_task("Finish project report", "Complete the report for the
client", "2023-12-01", 1, "2023-11-30 08:00")


    # Start the scheduler in a separate thread or process to run in the
background
```

```
print("Starting the automated task manager...")
run_scheduler()
```

Testing and Monitoring

1. **Run the Automated Task Manager**:
   - Start the script and add sample tasks.
   - Ensure the reminder checker runs daily and that alerts are sent correctly.
2. **Check Logs**:
   - Review task_manager.log for entries indicating successful reminders or errors.
3. **Test Different Scenarios**:
   - Try adding tasks with various due dates, checking that reminders and alerts trigger as expected.

Further Enhancements

1. **Graphical User Interface (GUI)**:
   - Build a GUI using Tkinter or a web framework to add, edit, and view tasks more easily.
2. **Enhanced Scheduling**:
   - Use the APScheduler library for more flexible scheduling, allowing reminders at specific intervals.
3. **Task Summaries and Reports**:

- o Add a function to generate weekly or monthly reports summarizing completed tasks and pending tasks.

4. **SMS Alerts**:
   - o Integrate Twilio for SMS alerts to make reminders even more effective for time-sensitive tasks.

5. **Advanced Data Analysis**:
   - o Use data analysis libraries to track task completion trends, helping users improve productivity over time.

In this chapter, we brought together various automation techniques to build a complete Automated Task Manager, incorporating database storage, scheduling, notifications, and logging. This project structure can be adapted for many other automation projects, providing a foundation for combining multiple tools and techniques into one cohesive solution.

In the next and final chapter, we'll discuss best practices for scaling automation projects, handling performance issues, and considerations for deploying automation in real-world environments.

AUTOMATE THE BORING STUFF WITH PYTHON

www.ingramcontent.com/pod-product-compliance
Lightning Source LLC
LaVergne TN
LVHW051324050326
832903LV00031B/3342